The Prairie Falcon

D1713269

NUMBER THIRTY-THREE
THE CORRIE HERRING HOOKS SERIES

Adult Prairie Falcon at eyrie. *Photo by Rick Kline*

STANLEY H. ANDERSON
JOHN R. SQUIRES

The Prairie Falcon

UNIVERSITY OF TEXAS PRESS
AUSTIN

Requests for permission to reproduce material from this work
should be sent to Permissions, University of Texas Press,
P.O. Box 7819, Austin, TX 78713-7819.

The paper used in this publication meets the
minimum requirements of American National Standard
for Information Sciences—Permanence of Paper for
Printed Library Materials, ANSI Z39.48-1984.

LIBRARY OF CONGRESS
CATALOGING-IN-PUBLICATION DATA

Anderson, Stanley H.
The prairie falcon / by Stanley H. Anderson and John R. Squires. — 1st ed.
    p.   cm. — (The Corrie Herring Hooks series ; no. 33)
Includes bibliographical references (p.   ) and index.
ISBN 0-292-70473-9 (alk. paper). — ISBN 0-292-70474-7 (pbk. : alk. paper)
    1. Prairie falcon.   I. Squires, John R.   II. Title.   III. Series.
QL696.F34A48   1997
598.9′18—dc20   96-41375

Contents

Preface and Acknowledgments

*F*or many years, we have been awed by the beauty and acrobatics of Prairie Falcons. During our many hours of research and bird watching, we have seen these birds courting, nesting, and capturing small birds and mammals. Sometimes we have seen them simply watching other birds and people approach their commanding perches. Other times we have also experienced these birds swooping down on us, just narrowly missing our heads.

It is exciting to watch the eggs hatch and the young grow and begin their life in flight. We look forward to banding the young and adult birds; it is always thrilling to handle these fascinating creatures. Perhaps the most pleasant part of all is simply sitting and watching Prairie Falcons from dawn to dusk and from season to season.

Our fascination with the Prairie Falcon has prompted us to write a book on this magnificent bird. Prairie Falcons are just as fascinating as their cousin the Peregrine Falcon; however, little has been written, in a popular form, about its life history.

Our purpose is to provide information to people interested in the Prairie Falcon and other birds of prey. In the first part of the book, we present observations on the Prairie Falcon's life history. We start by describing how it is related to other raptors. Then we examine the bird's behavior, interactions, and habitat. After discussing its characteristics, we describe its hunting habits and what it eats. Next, we follow the Prairie Falcon through the different seasons and describe their arrival on nesting areas, their courtship and nesting behavior. We also follow the young through their development and dispersal and discuss the information available on migration and winter ranges.

Finally, we look at people and the Prairie Falcon. We discuss falconry, especially as it relates to Prairie Falcons, examine the impact of pesticides and habitat destruction, and explore captive breeding and habitat mitigation. We then highlight a few of the many research projects on Prairie Falcons and how these studies help us understand this magnificent bird. In the appendix we discuss the etiquette everyone should observe when visiting Prairie Falcon nests.

We hope that this account of the Prairie Falcon excites your interest. We also hope that knowledge of and interest in the Prairie Falcon will aid in the conservation of this fascinating species.

Acknowledgments

We are indebted to many people who have studied the Prairie Falcon and heightened our interest in the bird. Tierny Parrish was of great assistance collecting literature for the book; Linda Ohler spent many hours helping on the word processor; Christine Waters helped with the index. Our wives, Donna Anderson and Chrisann Squires, provided valuable reviews.

The Prairie Falcon

Prairie Falcon hunting from perch. *Photo by Rick Kline*

CHAPTER I

The Prairie Falcon

I

THE BIRD

Journal Entry, 28 May 1984

Today we are attempting to trap Prairie Falcons on North
Butte, in Campbell County, Wyoming. We hope to attach radio
transmitters on nesting Prairie Falcons in order to study their
movements and habitat use. As we reach the cliff, winds are
light and the sun is just rising above the butte. Conditions are
perfect for trapping. The falcons are nesting on a 10-meter-
high cliff that rims the butte. By leaning far over the cliff edge,
we can see three pure white hatchlings huddled in the falcon's
eyrie. The down-covered young lack any feathering, so we estimate they are only one week old. Both adults spot us and begin to call while they circle high overhead. The adults grow
more agitated and dive repeatedly in an attempt to drive us
from their cliff. To capture the adults, we perch a live Great
Horned Owl near the eyrie and surround it with mist nets
hung from poles. Thus, when the falcons attack the owl, they
should become ensnared.

5:50 A.M.—The trap is set. The owl is calm, but the falcons
are nowhere in sight. We are hiding in a small grove of limber
pine approximately 100 meters from the trap. After a few minutes, we hear something that sounds like a sail ripping under
tension. Looking up, we discover the sound is coming from the
wind screaming through the feathers of a Golden Eagle as it
dives toward our owl. We immediately sprint toward the trap,
knowing the nets are not designed to capture Golden Eagles.
We fear for the owl's safety, but quickly realize the futility of
reaching the trap in time, so we stop and watch. Now only
70 meters away, it seems certain the eagle will crash through
the nets and kill the owl. At that same instant, we notice a male

Prairie Falcon diving toward the eagle. The falcon, which appears no larger than a dove compared to the massive eagle, is rapidly gaining on the eagle as it pumps its wings in a vertical stoop. The eagle, unaware of the approaching falcon, drops its talons as it plummets toward the owl. With astonishing speed, the falcon overtakes and strikes the eagle on its hind neck. The eagle with its talons still distended pulls up from its dive in staggered flight. The small falcon rebounds high over its eyrie, calling defiantly. . . .

Although we never captured any Prairie Falcons that day, we did renew our appreciation for their flying ability and indomitable courage. No other bird in the western United States matches a Prairie Falcon's aerobatic ability, except possibly its larger cousin, the Peregrine Falcon.

When people think about falcons, they often envision these legendary hunters dropping from the sky, attacking prey during high-speed stoops. The hunting prowess of falcons has fostered a kinship with humans throughout the centuries. Medieval kings and queens valued Peregrines, Gyrfalcons, and Merlins as courageous hunters, capable of killing quarry during high-speed chases. Prairie Falcons are also capable of high-speed attacks; at other times, Prairie Falcons simply drop from an elevated perch to grab a mouse.

Prairie Falcons have shared the open plains with Native Americans for centuries. Their feathers decorate the shields of ancient warriors, and falcon petroglyphs are a testament to Native Americans' respect for the species. Early settlers also watched Prairie Falcons as they drove their wagons across the high plains.

Prairie Falcons draw bird watchers, falconers, and, sadly to say, poachers, who feel it is sporting to shoot these magnificent creatures. Today, some populations are being subjected to illegal shooting and other activities, such as mining and development, that reduce their habitat and food supply.

Along with being very maneuverable and fast, Prairie Falcons can be quite aggressive. They may tolerate a Great Horned Owl's nesting nearby for several weeks and then suddenly attack the nest, killing the owl's young. These birds of the western plains are exciting to see during all seasons.

The Prairie Falcon is indeed a bird of contrasts. It can remain very quiet and complacent, blending into the background while perched in a tree or cliff. At other times, it can be a terror to its neighbors. When a falcon is unsuccessful in driving away an intruder, such as a human, it may mercilessly attack previously unmolested birds in order to vent its frustrations. Other birds nesting near breeding falcons may be left alone for long periods of time and then suddenly be subjected to a violent attack.

Prominent rocks near falcon eyries that are used as perch sites are often stained white from droppings. These "whitewash" areas can be seen from long distances and are frequently the first clue that falcons are present. Prairie Falcons readily defend their nest sites from intruders, occasionally striking and even drawing blood from persons venturing too close. More often, Prairie Falcons swoop within inches but rarely make contact. The swooshing sound of the wind through their feathers is usually convincing enough to frighten intruders to take cover. Attacking falcons show no mercy, whether a person or other animal is approaching the nest. Prairie Falcon's aggressive attacks on birds, such as barn owls and eagles, and on mammals, such as coyotes and fox, have all been successful in driving away intruders.

A Prairie Falcon researcher in Idaho, Anthonie Holthuizjen, observed thousands of aggressive interactions at thirty-seven nest sites. He found that each Prairie Falcon pair averaged six interactions per observation day. Aggressive attacks were highest just prior to egg laying. During incubation, the number of interactions declined but again increased about the time the eggs hatched. They declined again during early brood rearing but increased as the chicks aged. These interactions may be related to the amount of time falcons have available to perch and guard their territory.

Some Prairie Falcons may form pair bonds for life. This is based on studies that show the same pair of birds return to the same eyrie year after year. However, some females return to the eyrie each year with different mates. Other times, both pair members find a new mate. When a mate is lost during nesting or brood rearing, that bird is often replaced by a bird that was unable to breed because it lacked a territory.

Raptors

The general term *raptor* (from the Latin word *rapere,* meaning "one who seizes") includes all birds of prey. Raptors are flesh-eating birds that include falcons, hawks, vultures, eagles, and owls. Raptors typically have powerful feet with talons, hooked beaks, and keen eyesight for capturing and killing prey.

Falcons belong to the order Falconiformes, which also includes other diurnal birds of prey, such as eagles, hawks, buzzards, kites, harriers, ospreys, secretary birds, and condors. Falcons are classified in the genus *Falco,* which means they share certain characteristics that distinguish them from other raptors. Strigiformes consist of two families of owls, which are distinguished from other raptors by their large heads and forward directional eyes. The family Tytonidae includes 11 species of barn owl worldwide, whereas the family Strigidae includes 134 species of owls.

Vocalization

Prairie Falcons scream in a high-pitched voice. When birds approach their cliffs in the spring, they often emit a series of rapidly repeated *cacks,* or notes of varying pitches. Sometimes the notes are very spirited; others are very soft. Male *cacks* tend to be higher pitched than those of females. However, females and males cannot always be distinguished by their calls.

When people approach a nest site, the alarm note is a high, repeated *kee-kee-kee*, almost like a *cack*. Another note that the birds sometimes repeat is a rattling, such as a *kr-r-r-r*. Toward the end of this vocalization, the note often increases in volume. The birds also use another whining note called *kruk-kruk*. A distinct area around the nest is defended, and when intruders cross the line, the male or the female will emit alarm calls. While one member of the pair is vocalizing, the other may be swooping down, attacking the intruder. Other attacks may come without any type of vocalization whatsoever.

Coloration

Adult Prairie Falcons are found in several color phases—from light to dark with a series of gradations in between. Most of the time, the different color phases occur in different geographic areas. The exact reason for the color phases is not known.

At hatching, young Prairie Falcons are covered with a fine white down. In about two weeks, darker feathers appear, and after twenty-one days, noticeable feather tracts emerge. Recently fledged birds are colored dark above and light with speckles below, which is distinct from adults. Final plumage growth and the last shedding of down takes place at about two months of age as the young start to fly. At this stage the young falcons are buffier and more striped than the adults, with a more reddish tinge to the upper parts. The eye color of young falcons is brown, and their feet and legs are slate colored with black claws. The beak is bluish black, and a slight yellow tinge appears under the base of the mandible. The young assume a lighter color as they mature and are virtually identical to the adults by the end of the first summer.

Why Are Female Raptors
Typically Larger Than Males?

In most species of birds, males are larger than females. Charles Darwin believed this variance evolved through sexual selection as females chose larger males that were most competitive during contests for mates. However, in raptors the relationship is usually the opposite. Female raptors tend to be stronger, larger, and more dominant than males. This relationship is called "reversed size dimorphism," or simply "reversed dimorphism."

Reversed dimorphism apparently evolved under a predatory lifestyle, since it also arose independently in owls (Strigiformes), skuas (Stercorariinae), and in the various lineages within Falconiformes. Four of the five families of Falconiformes exhibit reversed dimorphism, including the Prairie Falcon. The one exception is the family containing the Secretary Bird, whose habits are more stork-like than raptorial. Reversed dimorphism also arose in frigate birds (Fregatidae) and boobies (Sulidae), which are both predatory foragers. The fact that reversed dimorphism evolved independently among so many different predatory lineages strongly suggests that it provides a significant adaptive advantage to predatory birds. The degree of reversed dimorphism varies from both sexes being equal in size, as with some kestrels, to females weighing twice as much as males (e.g., sharp-shinned hawks).

Ian Newton discovered that the degree of reversed dimorphism in raptors relates to their feeding habits. He identified seventy-five raptor species that feed on a single class of prey, such as insects, fish, mammals, or birds. Newton found that as the speed and agility of the prey increase, so does reversed dimorphism. Vultures and condors feeding on carrion show no consistent size differences between males and females, or if such differences occur, the males are larger than females. In snail feeders (e.g., snail kites), females are only slightly more dimorphic, followed by mammal and fish feeders. Raptors feeding on other birds are the most dimorphic of all.

Although the relationship between reversed dimorphism and prey agility is interesting in itself, it does not tell us why reversed dimorphism evolved or what advantage it offers predatory birds. Scientists have puzzled over this seemingly unanswerable question for a long time, resulting in at least fourteen proposed explanations for reversed dimorphism (see Mueller and Meyer 1985 for review). These diverse explanations (hypotheses) can be classified into three broad groups. Explanations in the first group assume that evolution favors larger-bodied females. Proposed advantages of larger females include a better ability to defend nests, improved egg incubation, larger egg production, better protection of egg follicles, better defense of the nest from male cannibalism, and domination of the male to force him to provide more food for the family. The second broad group of explanations argues that instead of females *increasing* in size, males *decreased* in size during their evolution. Small males have some advantages: they require less energy themselves, so more is available for the family; more prey is available to them than if they hunted large prey; and they may be more competitive when establishing territories compared with large males. The third group includes only a single explanation—the "dimorphic niche" hypothesis. This hypothesis contends that when males and females differ in size, the pair is better able to exploit a wider prey base. The diversity of these explanations indicates that no general agreement exists among raptor experts regarding the evolutionary forces causing reversed dimorphism. Although the "true" cause for dimorphism remains an enigma, some explanations are more plausible than others.

Some scientists believe that female dominance is the most important factor in the evolution of reversed dimorphism, probably because it facilitates and/or maintains the pair bond. However, other knowledgeable scientists believe the answer to this question rests on males becoming smaller, especially as this affects the pair's food requirements. Ydenberg and Forbes found that a decrease in male body size reduced daily energy required for flight (not carrying prey) by 40.7 percent. Small-bodied males reduce flight costs by 34.6 percent when carrying light loads and by 30 percent when carrying heavy prey.

The answer to the question, "Why are female raptors typically larger than males?" is still unknown. Although several plausible explanations exist, scientists will continue to investigate. New studies may eventually tip the balance of evidence toward a given theory. Meanwhile, the various attempts to answer this question illustrate that raptor biology is a dynamic science that often raises more questions than it answers.

Size

Male Prairie Falcons are 37–38 centimeters in length and weigh 500–635 grams. Females, on the other hand, are 45 centimeters in length and weigh 762–970 grams. Their wing span is up to 105 centimeters. Thus, observers can easily distinguish the male and the female in the field when both sexes are together.

Body Size and Life History

Ian Newton shows how various life-history parameters of raptors are correlated with body size. He points out that small raptors—kestrels, for example—usually mature early and often breed in their first year. They have large clutch sizes of four to six eggs and short breeding cycles of less than three months. Their life span is short, often less than ten years, and they have a fairly high annual mortality rate—40–50 percent. On the other hand, larger birds, such as condors, are slow to mature and often breed as late as five years of age. They typically have smaller clutch sizes, often consisting of only one egg, and longer breeding cycles, which take more than twelve months. The condor's life span is usually more than ten years and its mortality is generally low, around 5 percent. Medium-sized birds such as the Prairie Falcon show intermediate life-history characteristics.

Life-history strategies also impact population trends. Because of their high birth rate, populations of small-bodied species can quickly colonize an area if changes in nest sites or prey abundance become advantageous. On the other hand, the large-bodied raptors have a slow turnover and are usually more stable. They tend to select areas where the prey base is constant. Newton notes another trend: tropical raptors of equivalent size to temperate raptors have a lower breeding rate. Presumably, then, the tropical species also have a lower mortality rate, although data are lacking to substantiate this claim.

Thus, from a management perspective, larger birds that reproduce slowly are much more difficult to reintroduce into the wild than are small-bodied raptors. For example, the California Condor is near extinction due to pesticides, poisoning, and illegal shooting. The birds have been brought into zoos and have been laying eggs there successfully. However, it takes a great deal of time and effort to produce a large enough population of birds so that they can be reintroduced into the wild. By the same token, it takes a long time for these birds to colonize new areas in the wild. It may take several years after introduction before a population begins to breed. There are no breeding adults for them to successfully imprint on, and there are many environmental factors that could cause them harm.

Reintroduction of the Peregrine Falcon, which has a more intermediate life span, has been accomplished by placing nestlings (hacking) throughout the eastern and western United States. By feeding at release sites, young falcons are able to imprint on these areas. In some cases, they return and nest there the following year. This process has begun to establish a wild population. Prairie Falcons have also been successfully reintroduced, but not to the same degree as Peregrines. In order to establish reintroduced populations, breeding must continue over a period of years, eventually resulting in a surplus of adult birds. This surplus then allows adults that are killed to be replaced quickly by available birds in the population. Thus, a population of more long-lived birds may be harder to destroy; however, when they are all harmed over a period of years by pesticide poisoning or shooting, the population is extremely difficult to replace.

II

DISTRIBUTION AND NESTING SITES

Breeding Distribution

Prairie Falcons breed from southeastern British Columbia, southern Alberta, southern Saskatchewan, and northern North Dakota south to Baja California, southern Arizona, southern New Mexico, southeastern Coahuila, Mexico, western and northern Texas, and (formerly) northwestern Missouri. The states where Prairie Falcons are most abundant include Idaho, Wyoming, Utah, Montana, and California.

The southern extent of Prairie Falcon nesting is not well known. An immature Prairie Falcon was collected from an eyrie in the mountains of southeastern Coahuila, Mexico; this was the only nesting record for Mexico outside of Baja California. More recently, however, Prairie Falcons have been found nesting in the Sierra Madre Occidental Mountains in northeastern Mexico. Between 1975 and 1986, twenty-three Prairie Falcon eyries were located in northern Mexico. These falcons nested as far south as 23°30′ N latitude; there is little reason to believe this is the southern limit of the Prairie Falcon's nesting distribution. Additional fieldwork is needed to determine how far south Prairie Falcons nest in Mexico.

Nesting Density

The number of birds of prey that nest in a given area is usually determined by food availability and the abundance of nest sites. The number of suitable nest sites is particularly important in

Close-up of Prairie Falcon head. *Photo by Rick Kline*

determining the density of nesting Prairie Falcons. In the western United States, some open habitat contains few cliffs for Prairie Falcons to nest in, whereas other areas with an abundance of cliffs and rim rocks can support large concentrations of nesting Prairie Falcons.

Prairie Falcons tend to nest in the same area year after year. However, estimating the nesting density for such a wide-ranging species is difficult. Often, the resulting density estimates are quite crude. For example, Tom Cade has estimated that 5,000–6,000 Prairie Falcon pairs nest in the western United States and Canada (3.8–4.4 million square kilometers). It is hard to know the accuracy of density estimates over such a large land area. We would not be surprised if future research shows there are more pairs of Prairie Falcons than once believed.

Several western states have estimated the total numbers of nesting Prairie Falcons within their borders. In Wyoming, Bob Oakleaf estimates 800 pairs breed; Steve Platt estimates approximately 293–406 breeding pairs nest in New Mexico. Based on random sampling of suitable habitat, approximately 125 ± 94 pairs nest in western North Dakota, according to George Allen.

Biologists in California have expended much effort to determine the number of Prairie Falcons that nest in that state. Consulting with museums, ornithologists, falconers, egg collectors, and state and federal biologists from 1969 through 1972, they located a total of 218 Prairie Falcon territories. From 1970–1979, biologists using helicopters searched throughout California for additional Prairie Falcon eyries. They documented 1,250 nesting attempts at 520 different nesting territories. The current estimate is that 300–500 pairs of Prairie Falcons nest annually in California (764 square kilometers per territory) and fledge approximately 650–1,100 nestlings a year.

In California, Prairie Falcons were choosy about where they nest; not all habitats supported equal numbers of nesting Prairie Falcons. The Mojave Desert has the highest density of nesting birds (255 square kilometers per territory), whereas northwestern California supported the lowest (6,111 square kilometers per territory).

The greatest density of nesting Prairie Falcons is found in Idaho's Snake River Birds of Prey National Conservation Area. This area supports the world's largest concentration of nesting raptors—more than 600 pairs from fifteen different species nest in this area. In some years, more than 200 pairs of Prairie Falcons nest along the canyon walls at a density of 1 pair per 0.65 kilometers; this density represents the greatest concentration of nesting Prairie Falcons in the world. Falcons nest throughout the Snake River Canyon on nearly every suitable cliff. The higher the cliffs (120 meters or more), the greater the nesting density because Prairie Falcons nest above one another on the same cliff face.

As in California, the density of nesting Prairie Falcons in Idaho varies with habitat. Using a helicopter, biologists searched for nesting Prairie Falcons along Salmon Falls Creek, a deep river canyon in southern Idaho. Prairie Falcon nest densities varied from 0.05 nests per square kilometer to 0.31 nests per square kilometer, depending on the river section. More falcons nested along river sections bordered by sage bush and grass than sections bordered by agricultural lands. The density of Prairie Falcons may be affected by the varied abundance of small mammals that live near the canyon.

The nesting densities we have discussed only consider the number of breeding birds. However, it is important to realize that these same nesting areas also support surplus or non-breeding falcons. These non-territorial birds are always eager to take over territories when the resident Prairie Falcon is killed or is no longer able to defend its territory. The total size of the surplus population is unknown, but surplus birds form an important component in maintaining the stability of Prairie Falcon populations. For example, in western Wyoming, Doug Runde notes that surplus birds have replaced adult male or female resident birds that were killed during nesting. In some cases, the surplus bird actually moved in and assisted the remaining mate in raising the clutch of young nestlings. Whether or not the new mate returned to the site the next season is unknown.

Nesting in Trees

Prairie Falcons usually nest on cliffs, escarpments, or earthen slopes and prefer sites that offer overhead protection. There are two old records of Prairie Falcons nesting in trees. One record is from northwestern Missouri and the other is from southwestern Utah. In 1982, Trischa MacLaren and others observed a pair of Prairie Falcons engaging in courtship flights over a typical nest cliff. These falcons had fledged four young the previous year at the same site. MacLaren rechecked the site in May but found the site was unoccupied. However, on 15 June, MacLaren found a pair of Prairie Falcons vigorously defending a grove of ten ponderosa pine trees that were growing on a steep north-facing slope about 2 kilometers east of the nest cliff. Five of the trees contained old Black-billed Magpie nests in various states of disrepair. Atop one dilapidated magpie nest sat four downy young Prairie Falcons approximately two weeks of age. The nest was an open platform of sticks and mud located near the top of a 6-meter-tall pine tree. The development of these young was approximately two weeks behind the other pairs in the area. On 6 August, both adults and three young were observed flying near the pine grove.

MacLaren offered three possible explanations for these Prairie Falcons nesting in a tree. First, the adult falcons may have been disturbed at the nearby eyrie and were forced to move to the pine grove. This would explain why the phenology (or nesting cycle) of the tree-nesting falcons was later than other pairs. A second reason might have been that one pair member had fledged from a tree and was imprinted on tree-nesting sites. If the other pair member had resisted tree nesting, this could explain their delayed phenology. However, a shortage of traditional nest sites was not a factor, since acceptable sites were abundant in this area, including the unoccupied cliff site nearby. Finally, it was possible that the female was an immature bird, since immature birds tend to lay eggs later than adults. The mystery remains. No one will ever know why this pair picked such an odd nest site when traditional cliff sites could have been used. If a population of Prairie Falcons became tree nesters, they would be independent of cliffs and could possibly expand their range. But this is extremely unlikely given the historic reluctance of Prairie Falcons to nest in trees.

Occupancy and Nest-Site Fidelity

Cliff-nesting raptors like Prairie Falcons tend to use the same eyries year after year. It is often assumed the same individuals are faithful to both their territory and their mate. Some observations of unique individuals have reinforced this notion. For example, an albino female Prairie Falcon in Colorado nested at the same eyrie for nine years.

A desirable eyrie site will usually be used quickly by a new pair if the original pair does not return. The "white wash" from falcon excrement below some eyries can be seen for miles, apparently attracting falcons to the site. Prairie Falcons usually have several nest "potholes" or eyries located within their nesting territory. They frequently switch eyries from year to year but usually remain in the same territory.

In Idaho, approximately 97 percent of Prairie Falcon territories were occupied during a three-year study. In southwestern Wyoming, Douglas Runde visited 70–85 nesting territories per year from 1982 through 1986. He found that between 60 percent to 87 percent (mean 77 percent) of these eyries were occupied during any given year. Runde also summarized the results of eleven other Prairie Falcon studies and found that the mean occupancy rate for those studies was 74 percent (see Table 1). Thus, Prairie Falcons are indeed very traditional in using nest sites, but the results do not explain how consistent occupancy is maintained when birds die from time to time.

TABLE I

Occupancy Rates of Prairie Falcon Populations, 1966–1985

STUDY AREA AND DURATION	OCCU- PANCY RATE [a,b]	SOURCE
Alberta–Saskatchewan, 1966–68	69	Fyfe et al. 1969
Alberta, 1967–71	57	Edwards 1973
Colorado, 1969–70	85	Grater 1970
Colorado, 1976–78	87	Platt 1981
California, 1969–72	70	Garrett and Mitchell 1973
Idaho, 1975–78	83	U.S.B.L.M. 1979
Oregon, 1973–74	47	Denton 1975
Washington, 1971–72	87	Parker 1972 and 1973
Wyoming, 1980–85	57	Platt unpubl. data
Wyoming, 1982–84	91	MacLarren unpubl. data
Wyoming, 1982–85	83	Squires 1986
Unweighted Mean	74	

Source: Runde 1987.
[a] Percentage of occupied territories, or pairs producing young.
[b] Ninety-five percent confidence interval is 64–84%.

Doug Runde was particularly interested in determining whether or not breeding populations depend on locally produced young for recruitment or on young birds attracted from a larger regional population. But few studies have marked birds to see if the same individuals returned. Runde combined his results from Wyoming with studies in Alberta, Canada, and Colorado to describe Prairie Falcon turnover rate and mortality, dispersal distance, age structure, longevity, and site fidelity. Turnover is the change in individuals occupying breeding territories.

In all three studies, nesting Prairie Falcons were banded on breeding territories and were later recaptured in subsequent years. On territories where occupants were trapped in successive years (n=161), thirty-five individuals (22 percent) had changed territories by the next year. The turnover rate for males was 17 percent and 23 percent for females; the annual turnover rate for adults on territories was about 27 percent.

Sometimes adults will switch territories and find a new mate; other times, they may have simply died during the winter. Doug Runde found that the same adults used the same breeding territory for at least two breeding seasons about 80 percent of the time. Eight adults changed territories during Runde's study; five females moved from 0.2–3.9 kilometers, while three males moved 0.3–5.7 kilometers.

When a young Prairie Falcon is searching for a nesting territory of its own, it does not simply wander throughout the western United States. Usually, it searches for a suitable cliff eyrie near where it was born. This tendency is called phylopatry, and most raptors are phylopatric. For example, 76 percent of all banded European Sparrow Hawk recoveries were within 20 kilometers of their birthplace, and almost all were within 50 kilometers. The distance Prairie Falcons nest from their natal territories is not as well understood as it is for European Sparrow Hawks. In Idaho, most Prairie Falcons (71 percent) were sighted within 100 kilometers of their natal territories. Two of the females bred within 5–6 kilometers from their natal territories, whereas one male bird was 41 kilometers away.

Breeding near natal territories may benefit falcons because of their familiarity with their breeding areas. A detailed knowledge of the distribution of the food resource may be beneficial, especially for males that must feed their mate and their hungry

Close-up, front view of Prairie Falcon, adult. *Photo by Rick Kline*

brood. Hunting experience from previous years may help males locate prey concentration areas within their large hunting areas. In European Kestrels, nest-site fidelity changed from a peak of 70 percent when prey availability was high to a low of 10 percent when vole densities were low. It is unknown if territory quality also affects Prairie Falcon nest-site fidelity. Site fidelity in some raptors tends to be higher in males than females, and Prairie Falcon males and females may exhibit similar nest-site fidelity.

Nest-site fidelity has important implications for studies of raptor populations. The percentage of traditionally used and regularly revisited nest sites is one of the best measures of population trends. In Runde's study, the lower limit for nest-site fidelity was 81 percent. The probability that both surviving members of a pair nested elsewhere was low, estimated to be approximately 4 percent. This means the probability that nest vacancies were due to movements, rather than to mortalities, is less than 5 percent. Thus, trends in territory occupation should accurately reflect changes in the breeding population.

Tom Cade explains that "tradition" is an important factor linking generations of falcons to the same cliff. Continual use of a cliff is maintained as long as a new mate is attracted to a cliff when a pair member is lost. However, tradition for the territory is broken if both pair members die. The site may then remain unoccupied until rediscovered by a new pair of falcons.

It is important that Prairie Falcons continually reuse traditional nest sites so that a local falcon population persists. But human intervention can break nesting traditions and cause a local falcon population to vanish over time. For example, in the Central Valley of California, only one of thirty-three traditional Prairie Falcon eyries were occupied after large areas of native rangelands were converted to agricultural crops.

Territoriality

Nesting Prairie Falcons generally only defend the immediate area surrounding their nests from intruders. In northern California,

Prairie Falcons defended an area within 0.4 kilometers of their eyries; however, there were exceptions. At times, pairs nested within 90 meters of one another. In Wyoming, we have observed falcons nesting within 270 meters of each other with little defensive behavior. When pairs nest in close proximity, the eyries are typically visually isolated from adjoining territories by intervening ridges or canyon walls.

Foraging areas used by Prairie Falcons are normally located away from the eyrie and are not defended from other falcons. Radio-tagged Prairie Falcons use overlapping foraging areas, with little evidence of territorial defense. Aggressive interactions are usually limited to birds pirating prey from one another.

In contrast, at nest sites the ferocity of territorial attacks by Prairie Falcons varies from lethal strikes to total neglect. Early in the nesting season, when territorial fervor is especially high, one or both pair members may attack intruders with repeated stoops and vocalizations. Some of these territorial battles are prolonged. For example, four falcons (presumably two pairs) fought intermittently over a nest site for three days before the ownership dispute was settled. Nesting Prairie Falcons near Sunol, California, were observed defending their nest site from an intruding female Prairie Falcon. The resident male and female stooped repeatedly at the intruding female. At each attack, the intruder rolled upside down to present her talons. The intruder was pursued and harassed by the resident male, but she continued to make aerial advances toward the cliff face. The resident female appeared heavy and sluggish during the fray, suggesting she may have been carrying an egg. She perched on a ledge near her eyrie to watch the battle. Even though she was being aggressively pursued by the male, the intruding female landed next to the resident female. Both females faced off and screamed at each other; their bodies crouched in "horizontal threat displays." The resident female attacked, placing her head under the intruder's chest and lifting upward, forcing the intruder to take flight. The male then pursued her vigorously in a tail chase and ran her out of his territory. Upon returning to the nest cliff, the resident male and resident female copulated, and the female laid down on the nest scrape. Most territorial battles are not nearly as exciting.

Prairie Falcons nesting in the Snake River Birds of Prey Area rarely fight among themselves for eyries. Territorial limits along the cliffs are established early in the breeding season, and territorial boundaries are maintained by visual and vocal signals. To avoid conflicts falcons fly well above the cliff as they head for foraging areas.

As the nesting season progresses, Prairie Falcons become less defensive, sometimes allowing neighboring falcons to fly through their territories. Defensive behavior at the time of fledging is usually limited to brief chase flights or vocalizations. On several occasions in Wyoming, we saw two females from neighboring eyries sitting next to each other in a dead tree that had grown from the cliff's edge. The two falcons perched together for hours with no obvious territorial aggression, even when both adults had young. We also observed a radio-telemetered bird fly several miles to perch by another pair's eyries when young were present; again, territorial aggression was not apparent.

Prairie Falcons from adjacent territories have even helped resident falcons defend their site against approaching biologists. When people approach the eyrie, the resident pair usually swoops toward the humans, and often neighboring falcons then join in the defense.

Sometimes a resident pair may allow a second female to remain permanently in their nesting territory. At one site with three adults, both females helped the male defend the eyrie. The male copulated with both females, although only one brood was produced. No territorial aggression was apparent, and the second female was allowed within 3 meters of the nest by the other female. The male delivered prey to both females; all three adults remained at the eyrie until young were fledged.

Although territorial defense may be lax during the nesting stage, recently fledged falcons may be subjected to harsh attacks by neighbors, especially if they enter another pair's territory. Young fledglings can be struck and killed by neighboring adults. Examination of one such bird showed its skull had been crushed by the blow. Three other carcasses of recent fledglings, all with crushed skulls, were found in the area, suggesting they too were killed by neighboring adult falcons. However, nesting falcons do not always attack the nestlings from neighboring pairs. Mary McFadzen and John Marzluff observed a fledgling that moved 3.5 kilometers to another pair's territory after its nest mates were killed by a Great Horned Owl. This youngster perched and flew with the offspring from the adjacent pair for eleven days without suffering aggressive attacks from the adults; presumably, this fledgling was fed by neighboring adults during this period.

Home Ranges

A falcon's home range includes both nesting and foraging areas; however, as earlier noted, the birds only defend their nest site (territory). Delineating the size and shape of a home range for a mobile species like the Prairie Falcon is difficult. Early biologists depended on direct observations or recoveries of marked birds to determine home-range sizes. With the advent of radio telemetry, biologists now attach small radios to falcons to track their movements; relocations are then plotted on maps to determine the size and shape of the birds' home range.

Prairie Falcon home ranges vary in size according to habitat type and the abundance and distribution of prey. For example, in northern California, home ranges for nine falcons varied in size from 34 square kilometers to 389 square kilometers. The perimeter of these home ranges changed during the nesting season as falcons hunted different ecological groups of prey. In north-central Wyoming, we monitored the movements of six falcons and found their average home-range size was 112 square kilometers. In southern Idaho, the average home-range size for eighteen adult Prairie Falcons was 71 square kilometers, whereas

Prairie Falcons nesting in the Mojave Desert had a mean home-range size of 72 square kilometers for three males and 47 square kilometers for three females. The large size of Prairie Falcon home ranges indicates they must hunt over vast areas to provide food for nestlings.

Within the falcon's large home range are areas used consistently for foraging. We found that Prairie Falcons usually forage within 15 kilometers (linear distance) from their nest site. The distance of foraging habitats from the bird's eyrie is the most important factor affecting its use. Predictably, habitats close to the eyrie are more important than those far away. The second most important factor affecting where Prairie Falcons hunt is the degree of habitat openness. Important prey species such as Thirteen-lined Ground Squirrels may be most vulnerable in open habitat types. Bruce Haak also found that most falcon kills occurred in open habitats. In his California study area, cropland composed only 9 percent of the foraging habitat but was the site of 53 percent of the kills. Pasture composed 6 percent of the foraging habitat but was the site of 21 percent of the kills. Sagebrush was present on 71 percent of the foraging areas but was the site of only 1 percent of the kills. The results from both studies suggest that open habitats, such as grasslands within the home ranges, are very important to Prairie Falcons when hunting.

In Idaho's Snake River Birds of Prey National Conservation Area, John Marzluff, with the help of others, studied the ranging and habitat-use patterns of many individual Prairie Falcons (n=98). This area supports the greatest concentration of nesting Prairie Falcons in the world; roughly 200 pairs nest on 100 kilometers of cliffs bordering the Snake River. These falcons have very large home ranges that are approximately 29,757 hectares (115 square miles). The large size of these home ranges results from the patchy distribution of habitats that support prey populations; especially important are habitats that support Townsend's Ground Squirrels. In years of normal rainfall, ground squirrels are most abundant in native bunchgrass and bluegrass habitats. During drought years, ground squirrels survive better in native sagebrush and around agricultural fields. Falcons appear to select home ranges based on the presence of good squirrel habitat. Falcons with access to the best home ranges—those containing the highest percentage of bluegrass, sagebrush, and winterfat (*Ceratoides lanata*)—range over significantly smaller areas than the ranges used by pairs nesting further from these habitats. Home-range size is an important consideration because it affects productivity.

Prairie Falcons experience a "cost" associated with ranging over very large home ranges. In Idaho, Marzluff found that Prairie Falcons cannot range more than 300 square kilometers and still provide food and protection to nestlings. When falcons had to travel over home ranges 350–400 square kilometers in size, they experienced poor reproduction; conversely, they enjoyed good reproduction when their home ranges were only 200 square kilometers. Similarly, falcons that nest in areas that support poor prey populations have to range over larger areas than birds that nest near good squirrel habitat. Thus, the conversion of native rangeland habitat to exotic cheatgrass that supports poor prey populations can reduce Prairie Falcon productivity. John Marzluff's work is particularly good at illustrating how changes in vegetation impact prey populations and how these changes in turn influence Prairie Falcon populations. In other words, all components in the rangeland ecosystem are interrelated and all links of the food chain are needed if viable Prairie Falcon populations are to be maintained.

During the winter, Prairie Falcons may use home ranges that are much smaller than home ranges used during nesting. Winter home ranges average approximately 30 square kilometers (12.3–68.0 square kilometers). In north-central Colorado, Jim Enderson estimated the maximum dimension across winter home ranges was 9 kilometers. The size of these winter home ranges seems very small, considering falcons can cover this distance in less than a few minutes. Apparently, small home ranges are adequate for providing food to lone wintering birds, compared to the large summer home ranges that are necessary when adults must feed hungry broods.

III
HUNTING AND FOOD HABITS

The hunting ability and food habits of Prairie Falcons are important factors to consider when trying to understand their biology. Food habits affect all aspects of raptors' life histories—where they winter, their daily activity patterns, and the number of young they produce.

Equipped for Hunting

Prairie Falcons are well adapted to their lifestyle of high-speed chases, rapid dives, and rough-and-tumble battles when dispatching prey. They possess many obvious hunting adaptations, such as gripping feet armed with talons and a sharp bill for killing and consuming prey. Other adaptations are not obvious. Prairie Falcons, like most raptors, depend on their vision for locating prey. The eyeballs of falcons are proportionally fifteen times larger than the eyes of humans. Larger eyeballs produce large, clear images. Large eyes also allow maximum cornea dilation for capturing the greatest amount of available light. Prairie Falcons have eyes that are proportionally larger than those of other falcons, but the adaptive significance of such large eyes is unknown. The sharp curvature of the eyes of raptors places the image-sensitive retina far from the lens, forming a long focal length or slightly telescopic vision. Their retinas are also packed with millions of color-sensitive cone cells; these cells are most concentrated in the two fovea, the most sensitive areas of the retina (see Figure 1).

The eye of most diurnal raptors contains both a lateral and a central fovea, which allows for their extreme visual acuity. The central fovea facilitates monocular vision, whereas the lateral

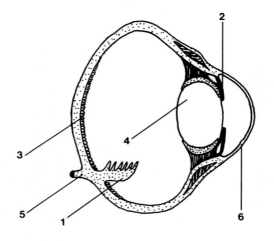

FIGURE 1A
Cross section of
falcon eye

1. Pecten	*3. Retina*	*5. Optic nerve*
2. Iris	*4. Lens*	*6. Cornea*

FIGURE 1B
Cross section of falcon head showing location
of eye and picture of pecten

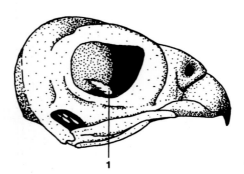

1. Pecten

*Redrawn after Johnsgard (1990), Hawks, eagles, and falcons
of North America, Smithsonian Institution Press (after Grassé [1950], fig. 5a and d).*

Flying adult Prairie Falcon showing field marks. *Photo by Rick Kline*

fovea relates to binocular vision. The eyes of Prairie Falcons are set forward, allowing for excellent depth perception that is necessary when rapidly pursuing prey. Prairie Falcons also have well-developed neural connections behind their eyes, allowing for complex image processing.

The eyes of raptors contain a small structure called a pecten, which is a pleated, blood-filled protrusion (see Figure 1). The function of this structure is not well understood. It is smallest in nocturnal birds, a little larger in seed eaters, larger still in insectivores, and largest of all in birds of prey. The pecten provides nutrients to the eye and may assist with detecting movement.

Prairie Falcons also have a distinctive "eyebrow" or superciliary ridge over the eye, giving them their hawk-like appearance.

The superciliary ridge and associated feathering may shade the eye from the sun's glare, allowing them to clearly see prey under bright conditions. The superciliary ridge may also protect the eye from physical damage from blows to the head or shield the eye from wind and dust during flight. Most falcons, including Prairie Falcons, also have black mustachial stripes near the eyes that may further reduce glare.

Falcons, like other diurnal raptors, have good but not exceptional hearing. In this they differ sharply from owls, whose exceptional hearing allows them to hunt using auditory rather than visual cues. Owls have eyes that function extremely well in low light but are not extraordinary in terms of absolute visual acuity. In contrast, falcons have high visual acuity and unspecialized hearing, consistent with their reliance on visual rather than auditory means to locate prey.

Prairie Falcons have long, narrow wings that are shaped in a manner reflecting their foraging strategy. The outer three feathers of a falcon's wing are the longest primaries and lack pronounced emarginations. Some raptors have primaries that act as individual wing slots during flight. For example, soaring hawks (buteos) and eagles have broad round-tipped wings, with the third and fourth primaries the longest flight feathers. Their primaries have pronounced emarginations that, when spread during flight, minimize turbulence while maximizing lift. In addition, the wings of soaring raptors are large relative to their body weight (i.e., a low wing loading). This adaptation allows buteos and eagles to soar effortlessly for long periods when foraging. In contrast, falcons have heavy wing loadings and usually flap their wings rapidly when flying. Heavy wing loadings allow Prairie Falcons to attain extremely high speeds when stooping on prey.

Hunting Techniques

When we visualize a hunting falcon, we think of spectacular dives and high-speed chases. However, this stereotype is often inaccurate. Birds in the genus *Falco* have a great diversity of hunting styles. Large-bodied falcons, like Peregrines or Gyrfalcons, often stoop on avian prey such as pigeons, ducks, or grouse and knock them from the sky or grip and force them to the ground. Species of Hobby Falcons hunt birds and insects at great heights, whereas Eleonora's Falcons specialize in pursuing migrant birds. Merlins often hunt small birds with their wings low, tail chasing and eventually overtaking their intended quarry. American Kestrels often hover when hunting insects and mice but, at other times, may chase flocks of goldfinches with Merlin-like zeal. Even within a species, hunting styles change according to prey type, weather conditions, and habitat characteristics.

Prairie Falcons usually hunt by rapidly flying 10–60 meters above the ground in an attempt to locate unwary prey, followed by a direct glide to the quarry. Prairie Falcons sometimes fly much lower, approximately 5 meters from the ground, using a low, flushing flight pattern. Bruce Haak studied nesting Prairie Falcons in California and observed they normally used a low-course attack. These falcons ended their stoops at the perimeter of a field and had generated sufficient momentum for the birds to glide more than 1 kilometer only three feet above the ground. This low, flat flight profile makes it difficult for prey to see the falcon in time to escape.

The attack styles used by Prairie Falcons wintering at Beaverhill Lake, Alberta, can be characterized into one of three categories. During sunny or windy weather, hunting falcons will soar as high as 100 meters above the ground. After sighting prey, they pull in their wings and dive at 30–60° angles as they plummet toward the ground. When they approach their intended quarry, they level off near the ground and rapidly glide the last 10 to 300 meters without flapping their wings. The second style of Prairie Falcon attack is best described as an "oblique descent from flapping flight." During these attacks, the falcon flies at low altitudes (10–150 meters) and then suddenly descends in an oblique or shallow dive that is sufficient to rapidly increase its flight speed when attacking quarry. "Opportunistic low flight" is a third flight pattern used by Prairie Falcons at Beaverhill Lake. Falcons using this hunting technique fly low along the ground, attempting to seize any prey flushed by their sudden appearance. Of the forty-four attacks observed at Beaverhill Lake, all were directed toward prey on the ground or in shallow water.

Although the hunting techniques described at Beaverhill Lake are typical, Prairie Falcons sometimes hunt like accipiters (forest hawks). Accipiters, such as Cooper's Hawks or Goshawks, use low and concealed, hedge-hopping flights when ambushing their prey. Prairie Falcons can use a very similar hunting strategy. For example, after sitting on a pole for a few minutes, a falcon was seen flying to a height of 35 meters toward a circling flock of starlings that were more than a kilometer

Flying adult Prairie Falcon showing field marks. *Photo by Rick Kline*

away. After flying at this height for 200 meters, the falcon dropped down very low, skimming the tops of sagebrush and fences. It sped under several trees and along a fence row until it was directly under the starlings. The falcon then turned nearly 80° directly upward into the flock and tried to grab starlings with both feet, but the attempt failed. The bird perched on another pole for a few minutes, then launched a similar attack in a new direction on prey unseen by the observer. Five minutes later, the Prairie Falcon returned, clutching a starling in its foot.

Sometimes Prairie Falcons hunt like Northern Harriers (Marsh Hawks), using a low, slow, but highly maneuverable flight. An immature Prairie Falcon was observed almost hovering over clumps of vegetation, apparently trying to flush small rodents and birds. Prairie Falcons also hunt directly with harriers. They fly approximately 30–50 meters above and 50–100 meters behind harriers as they course across open fields. The falcon then stoops on the birds flushed by the harrier.

When driving across western rangelands, one can often see Prairie Falcons perching on utility poles or towers. Hunting from tall perches is called "still hunting" and is frequently used by Prairie Falcons. When prey is seen, the falcon dives from the perch and flies rapidly, close to the ground, for approximately 400 meters before it glides the last few yards of its attack.

Since successful hunting is a matter of life or death for Prairie Falcons, they are highly opportunistic. We spent one afternoon watching a male Prairie Falcon (male falcons are called tiercels) hunt Cliff Swallows that were nesting approximately 50 meters from the bird's eyrie. Cliff Swallows build mud nests that they attach to cliff walls. The tiercel circled approximately 100 meters over the swarm of swallows while they busily fed their young. Suddenly, he plunged through the flock of panicked swallows, attempting to snatch one during his pass. After the attack, the tiercel left the area for approximately ten minutes, allowing the swallows to resume feeding their young before it launched another attack. On several occasions, the tiercel actually hung upside down from a swallow's mud nest with one talon while reaching inside with the other, trying to grab the young nestlings. The falcon did not capture any swallows during these attempts, but other biologists have seen Prairie Falcons successfully use similar hunting techniques when hunting Cliff Swallows.

Prairie Falcons also imitate the flight patterns of other birds in an apparent attempt to deceive potential prey. In Nevada, a pair of Prairie Falcons was observed imitating the undulating flight pattern of Loggerhead Shrikes. This hoax enabled the falcons to approach within 10 meters of White-tailed Antelope Squirrels before they became alarmed. When the squirrels realized their mistake and began to run, the falcon rushed forward in a direct attack.

Prairie Falcons will readily take prey from other raptors (kleptoparasitism) when given the opportunity. Early one morning in May, we parked our truck to scan a cliff for nesting Prairie Falcons. A Northern Harrier flew up and killed a mouse in a grassy area less than 25 meters from our truck. Immediately, a male falcon began calling from the cliff and then stooped at the harrier. At the last minute, the harrier jumped into the air, dropping its mouse as it flew away. The falcon retrieved his stolen prey and quickly flew back to the cliff to eat. We also watched a male falcon attack a Northern Harrier when it flew past its eyrie, forcing it to drop its prey. The falcon recovered the prey and fed it to its young.

While fly fishing the Frying Pan River in western Colorado, Harold Webster observed a Prairie Falcon pirate prey from a Peregrine Falcon. The Prairie badgered the adult Peregrine in an attempt to force it to drop a freshly caught bird. After several stoops in which both birds apparently made contact, the Peregrine finally dropped its prey. After catching the prey in midair, the Prairie flew directly to her eyrie to feed her hungry brood.

Although Prairie Falcons are relentless hunters that are capable of using many different hunting styles, their prey have a few tricks of their own to foil an attacking falcon. Bruce Thompson and James Tabor were driving down a road in

Washington state when a female Mallard suddenly appeared, flying very close to the roadway. The Mallard flew near to the car and then swooped off. Within two or three seconds, a Prairie Falcon dove at the duck. The bird aborted its attack as the Mallard continued to fly about 1–4 meters above the highway surface, weaving to the left and right between several cars. Finally, the falcon hit the duck, causing it to tumble to the ground on the side of the highway. The downed duck then crawled under a sagebrush. The falcon made several other swoops but the duck remained safe.

Prairie Falcons sometimes kill more prey than they immediately consume. They often hide these prey items in clumps of grass, sagebrush, or other brushy vegetation that grow on ledges or in cavities near their eyries. Food caching is probably a universal behavior among falcons and has been documented for the following species: Peregrine, Gyrfalcon, Prairie Falcon, Bat Falcon, Aplomado Falcon, New Zealand Falcon, Merlin, Eleonora's Falcon, Common Kestrel, and American Kestrel. Caching is most frequent during the breeding season, but some species cache throughout the year.

Anthonie Holthuijzen studied the caching behavior of Prairie Falcons in southwestern Idaho. Just before thrusting the prey into a hiding place, the falcon would carefully scan its surroundings to make sure other birds were not watching. Potential cache robbers, especially crows and their allies, are driven off before the food is cached. Prairie Falcons cache the greatest number of prey items during brood rearing, especially when the young are only 0–3 days of age. At this age, young nestlings need to be fed frequently but cannot eat more than a few morsels during a given feeding. Females are usually responsible for hiding prey; males only cached food when the females were absent or when the young did not eat the prey.

Prairie Falcons usually retrieve their cached food items just after sunrise. Nestlings are particularly hungry at this time, because they have been without food during the night. Retrieval rates may also peak again in the early evening. Caching food has the obvious advantage of providing nourishment during periods when capturing sufficient prey may be impossible. This behavior dampens the variation in food availability, which is especially important to Prairie Falcons during brood rearing.

What Do Prairie Falcons Eat?

Prairie Falcons eat a wide variety of prey (see Table 2), mostly consisting of small birds and mammals. The actual species composition of the falcons' diet depends on local prey availability and individual hunting ability, both of which are highly variable. For example, some Prairie Falcons forage extensively on birds, whereas other populations depend largely on mammals (see Table 2). In Idaho, Mary McFadzen and John Marzluff observed that Prairie Falcons delivered fewer Townsend's Ground Squirrels during years of low squirrel abundance but instead shifted their diet to include more birds and reptiles (3 percent birds and reptiles during years of high squirrel abundance versus approximately 16–19 percent during years of low squirrel abundance). Prairie Falcons usually hunt in early morning or late afternoon. During midday, particularly if it is hot, the falcon often remains in a shaded roost or nest site, although the birds can sometimes be seen soaring during this period.

The well-known American ornithologist A. C. Bent reported that Prairie Falcons have eaten Brewer's Blackbirds, English Sparrows, Chestnut-collared Longspurs, Yellow-headed Blackbirds, doves, quail, pigeons, Sharp-tailed Grouse, coot, Mallards, Teal, and even domestic chickens. He reported that Western Meadowlarks and Mourning Doves were also popular food choices of the Prairie Falcon.

Although Prairie Falcons eat a diversity of foods, some types of prey are important to many populations. For example, mammalian prey are an important dietary component of most Prairie Falcon populations, especially during nesting. Preferred small mammal prey include Richardson's Ground Squirrel, Thirteen-lined Ground Squirrel, Wyoming Ground Squirrel,

TABLE 2

Prairie Falcon Food Habits in the Western United States

SOURCE AND AREA	PREY COMPOSITION
Haak 1982 California	Percent of captioned individuals: 41% Belding's ground squirrel, 45% vole, 3% horned lark, 3% cedar waxwing.
Becker 1979 Montana	Mammals: including Thirteen-lined Ground Squirrel, Least Chipmunk, Northern Pocket Gopher, and Whitetail Prairie Dog. Birds: including Western Meadowlark, Mountain Blue-bird, Lark Bunting, Rock Dove, Vesper Sparrow, American Robin, Common Flicker, Brewer's Blackbird, Horned Lark, American Kestrel, Red-winged Blackbird, Killdeer, Sharp-tailed Grouse, Mourning Dove, Pinyon Jay, Black-billed Magpie, Loggerhead Shrike, and Poor Will. Total diet was composed of 22.8% mammals and 77.2% birds.
Bent 1937[a] Montana	Mammals: prairie dogs, ground squirrels, tree squirrels, pocket gophers, mice, jack rabbits, other rabbits. Birds: mallards, teals, other ducks, Sharp-tailed Grouse, prairie chickens, Gambel's Quail, Ring-necked Pheasants, Gray Partridge, domestic poultry, coots, waders, gulls, Band-tailed Pigeons, Rock Doves, Mourning Doves, jays, House Sparrows, meadowlarks, Yellow-headed Blackbirds, Brewer's sparrows, White-crowned Sparrows, and Chestnut-collared Longspurs. Reptiles, including lizards. Invertebrates: grasshoppers, crickets, and other insects.

TABLE 2 (*continued*)

SOURCE AND AREA	PREY COMPOSITION
Boyce 1985 Mojave Desert, California	Mammals: California Ground Squirrel, Mojave Ground Squirrel, White-tailed Antelope Squirrel, Valley Pocket Gopher, Pocket Mouse, Kangaroo Rat, Desert Woodrat, Black-tailed Jack Rabbit, and Desert Cottontail. Birds: Chukar, Western Sandpiper, Rock Dove, Mourning Dove, White-throated Swift, Western Kingbird, Say's Pheobe, Horned Lark, Cactus Wren, Rock Wren, Sage Trasher, Lecont's Trasher, Mountain Bluebird, Loggerhead Shrike, European Starling, Black-headed Grosbeak, White-crowned Sparrow, Western Meadowlark, Red-winged Blackbird, Brewer's Blackbird, Scott's Oriole, Northern Oriole, Western Tanager, House Sparrow, and House Finch. Reptiles: Desert Iguana, Chuckwalla, Zebra-tailed Lizard, Desert Horned Lizard, and Western Whiptail. Overall diet composition was 52% mammals, 38% birds, and 10% reptiles.
Brown and Amadon 1968[a]	Small and medium-sized birds and mammals. Rarely ants and large insects.
Denton 1975[a] Oregon	Mammals: Townsend's Ground Squirrel, Belding's Ground Squirrel, Golden-Mantled Ground Squirrel, and Least Chipmunk. Birds: including Mourning Dove, Horned Lark, Starling, Western Meadowlark, and Red-winged Blackbird.
Enderson 1964[a] Colorado	Richardson's Ground Squirrels, Thirteen-lined Ground Squirrels, White-throated Swift, Black-billed Magpie, Loggerhead Shrike, Western Meadowlark, Vesper Sparrow, and McCown's Longspur.

Holthuijzen 1990 Idaho	Townsend's Ground Squirrel was the most common prey item and was present in 37% of food items, followed by other small mammals (27.1%), birds (4.0%), and lizards (0.7%).
Leedy 1972[a] Montana	Richardson's Ground Squirrel and Mountain Cottontail, Horned Lark, Western Meadowlark, Vesper Sparrow, Black-billed Magpie, and Brewer's Blackbird.
MacLaren et al. 1988 Wyoming	Mammals: Wyoming Ground Squirrel (59%), Leporidae (6.5%), Thirteen-lined Ground Squirrel (1.2), and White-tailed Prairie Dog (19%). Birds occurred in 13.7% of samples. The diet in terms of biomass was 98.4% mammalian prey and 1.6% avian.
Marti and Braun 1975[a] Colorado	Mammals: Yellow-bellied Marmot, Golden-mantled Ground Squirrel, Northern Pocket Gophers, Deer Mice, Long-tailed Voles, and Pikas. Birds: Ptarmigan, Horned Larks, Mountain Bluebirds, Water Pipits, and Rosy Finches. Total diet was composed of 39.3% mammals and 60.7% birds.
McKinley, unpublished[a] Colorado	Mammals: Thirteen-lined Ground Squirrels and Richardson's Ground Squirrel. Birds: Horned Larks, Western Meadowlarks, Mourning Doves, Lark Sparrow, Blue Jay, Brewer's Blackbirds, and Common Nighthawk. Diet was composed of 55.3% mammals and 44.7% birds.
Ogden 1973[a] Idaho	Mammals: Townsend's Ground Squirrel, White-tailed Antelope Squirrel, Kangaroo Rats, Woodrats, and Desert Cottontail. Birds: Horned Larks, California Quail, Chukar, Ring-necked Pheasant, Rock Dove, Mourning Dove, Burrowing Owl, nighthawks, Cliff Swallow, Rock Wren, Starling, Western Meadowlark, Red-winged Blackbird, and Western Tanager.

TABLE 2 (*continued*)

SOURCE AND AREA	PREY COMPOSITION
	Reptiles include Collared Lizard, Leopard Lizard, Horned Lizard, and Spotted Whiptail. Invertebrates: grasshoppers and scorpions.
Platt unpublished[a] New Mexico	Mammals: Thirteen-lined Ground Squirrel, Spotted Ground Squirrels, Plains Pocket Gophers, Kangaroo Rats, and Desert Cottontail. Birds: Scaled Quail, Mourning Doves, Lewis' Woodpecker, Horned Larks, Western Meadowlarks. Invertebrates included beetles. Diet composition was 65.6% mammals, 32.8% birds, and 1.5% invertebrates.
Porter and White 1973[a] Utah	Mammals: Uinta Ground Squirrels, Rock Squirrels, and vole. Birds: ducks, California Quail, Ring-necked Pheasants, American Avocets, Killdeer, Willets, Sanderling, Rock Dove, Mourning Dove, Common Flicker, Western Kingbird, Horned Lark, robins, House Sparrow, Western Meadowlarks, Brewer's Blackbird, and Rufous-sided Towhees. Mammals composed 7.9% and birds 92.1% of the diet.
Smith and Murphy 1973[a] Utah	Mammals: White-tailed Antelope Squirrel, Deer Mouse, Black-tailed Jackrabbits. Birds: Horned Larks, European Starlings, Western Meadowlark, Green-tailed Towhee, and Vesper Sparrow. Invertebrates include locusts. Overall diet was composed of 30.8% mammals, 50% birds, and 19.2% invertebrates.
Squires et al. 1989 Wyoming	Fifteen species of prey were utilized by nesting Prairie Falcons as determined through pellet analysis. Thirteen-lined Ground Squirrels, the

most common prey, were present in 91% of the
pellets, followed by 56% Meadow Larks, 23%
Horned Larks, and 12% Lark Buntings. The
remaining prey species were present in low
frequencies ($\leq$5%). Eighty-nine percent of
pellets contained both bird and mammal
remains. Four percent of pellets contained
only bird remains, while 7% contained only
mammalian remains.

Voilker, unpublished[a] Oklahoma	Mammals included Rock Squirrels. Birds include Scaled Quail, Mourning Dove, Black-billed Magpie, and meadowlark. Diet was composed of 8.4% mammals and 91.6% birds.

[a]As reported in Sherrod 1978.

Townsend's Ground Squirrel, Belding's Ground Squirrel,
Golden-mantled Ground Squirrel, Least Chipmunk, California
Ground Squirrel, Mojave Ground Squirrel, and white-tailed
Antelope Squirrel. These rodents are active during the day
when falcons are foraging, and their small size makes them easy
prey for male Prairie Falcons.

Small birds are also important prey for Prairie Falcons. Important avian prey include Horned Larks, Lark Buntings,
Mourning Doves, Western Meadowlarks, and a variety of blackbirds. Western Meadowlarks are particularly desirable prey for
nesting Prairie Falcons. In northeastern Wyoming, we found
that 56 percent of regurgitated pellets from Prairie Falcons contained Western Meadowlarks, 23 percent contained Horned
Larks, and 12 percent contained Lark Buntings. Western Meadowlarks were the primary avian prey, even though eight other
species of birds were more numerous on falcon foraging areas.
Other biologists have also found that Meadowlarks are an important prey item (see Table 2).

Horned Lark is an important food item for Prairie Falcons, especially during the winter. Doug Boyce found Horned Lark remains in 63 percent of the Prairie Falcon eyries in the Mojave Desert in California; other biologists have found Horned Larks to be important prey as well (see Table 2). Jim Enderson conducted some of the earliest studies on the distribution of wintering Prairie Falcons in southern Wyoming and northern Colorado. Horned Lark was the only species of prey that was strongly related to the abundance of wintering Prairie Falcons. At the onset of winter, Horned Larks begin flocking together in groups of fifty or more birds. These flocks then move to low-elevation agricultural areas to feed on winter wheat. As the number of Horned Larks increased in agricultural areas, so did the number of wintering Prairie Falcons. On several occasions, falcons were observed hunting Horned Larks.

Gary Beauvais and his associates observed wintering Prairie Falcons attack prey on forty different occasions. All but two attacks were directed toward Horned Larks. Attacks on Horned Larks were only successful 13.5 percent (n = 37) of the time. Most attacks (65 percent) were on flocks of Horned Larks that exceeded fifty individuals. Large flocks of Horned Larks are associated with cultivated lands, which in turn attract wintering Prairie Falcons.

Although the Prairie Falcon's diet mostly comprises small birds and mammals, it occasionally includes unusual prey items. For example, Doug Boyce found that Prairie Falcons ate reptiles, which compose up to 9.5 percent of their diet. Desert Horned Lizard and Chuckwalla were found in 20 percent of the Mojave Desert nests, where a Prairie Falcon was also seen flying down from a power pole to kill a snake. Insects can also be an important food source, depending on the abundance of other prey (see Table 2).

While studying the food habits of Prairie Falcons nesting near Gillette, Wyoming, we found one pellet composed entirely of Mule Deer hair. We believe there are at least two explanations for such an unusual food item. The falcon could have fed on deer carrion directly or may have eaten the stomach of a carrion-feeding bird (e.g., Pinyon Jay, Clark's Nutcracker, Brewer's Blackbird). The deer-hair pellet contained no feather remains, suggesting the falcon fed directly on carrion. To our knowledge, this is the first circumstantial evidence of Prairie Falcons consuming carrion.

We also found a pellet composed entirely of the shells of aquatic snails, without any trace of feather or fur remains. It is difficult to envision how a Prairie Falcon would encounter snails when foraging. Possibly, the falcon ate the stomach of an aquatic-feeding bird (i.e., Killdeer or waterfowl) that contained shells, but this seems unlikely since the pellet lacked feather remains. The falcon might have selectively picked snails from the aquatic vegetation while drinking or bathing. Other birds eat snails to help meet their calcium requirements for egg production. Perhaps Prairie Falcons are similar in this behavior.

Cannibalism of chicks has been documented for Prairie Falcons. On one occasion, a female falcon plucked a dead twenty-six-day-old chick and fed the carcass to herself and the two remaining chicks. After several minutes, she flew from the eyrie to the ground and continued to feed before flying off with the remains. Biologists commonly discover eyries where chicks have died but no remains are found. Possibly, scavengers such as ravens or crows are responsible for eating dead chicks, but this explanation seems unlikely because the adults often aggressively defend the eyrie, even when chicks have recently died. Cannibalization of dead chicks may be more common than once thought.

Although we have seen that Prairie Falcons feed on diverse prey, they are fairly specialized in terms of their overall diet. The diet of Prairie Falcons from any one area usually consists of a few dominant prey types. Patricia MacLaren along with other researchers studied the food habits of Golden Eagles, Red-tailed Hawks, Prairie Falcons, and Ferruginous Hawks near

Medicine Bow, Wyoming. She found that the Prairie Falcon was the most specialized raptor, feeding primarily on prairie dogs and ground squirrels.

Karen Steenhof and Mike Kochert studied the diets of Golden Eagles, Red-tailed Hawks, and Prairie Falcons in southwestern Idaho. They, too, found that Prairie Falcons had the most specialized diet; Red-tailed Hawks had the most diverse diet. None of these three species of raptors merely selected the most abundant prey. Instead, each concentrated its predation on certain species based on size. Golden Eagles primarily ate larger prey, like Black-tailed Jackrabbits; Red-tailed Hawks and Prairie Falcons preferred to eat smaller rodents, such as Townsend's Ground Squirrels. All three raptors switched to less desirable quarry when their preferred prey became scarce.

Behavioral characteristics may favor a raptor becoming a dietary specialist or a generalist. For example, Red-tailed Hawks live in small, well-defended territories and spend more time searching for rather than pursuing prey. They also encounter a diversity of prey during their long winter migrations. As a result, Red-tailed Hawks are generalists, taking whatever they find. In contrast, Prairie Falcons have more specialized diets because they forage in very extensive territories. They pursue select prey items rather than search for and take whatever they see. Specialists such as Prairie Falcons depend on prey that are available from year to year.

How Do Biologists Know What Falcons Eat?

The food that falcons eat affects all aspects of their life histories. It influences where they nest, what habitats they use, and when they will be active. Scientists primarily use five methods to determine raptor diets. The first method involves collecting the raptor and identifying its stomach contents. This method allows scientists to identify smaller, more easily digested prey items that other techniques might miss. It was used by early scientists who killed hawks to determine the diets of "good" and "bad" raptors. Killing raptors just to determine their diets can rarely be justified, so few scientists would use this method today.

The second method involves squeezing food from the crop and back out the mouths of nestlings to examine their diets. This technique does yield valuable diet information during nesting but should be performed with caution and with proper permits. Potential problems may include damage to esophageal tissue from sharp bones in the crop and a decrease in nutrients to young. Of course, we must always be cautious when working around a Prairie Falcon eyrie, as our odor may attract mammalian predators after we leave.

The third technique for determining food habits is through direct observation, usually from a blind constructed near the nest. Researchers use spotting scopes to identify prey items as the parents feed their young. Although scientists often use direct observation when identifying raptor foods, this procedure often requires hundreds of hours of field observation to gather sufficient data. In addition, many raptors pluck their prey before returning to the nest, so identifying some food items is difficult, if not impossible.

Searching nests or plucking perches for prey remains is the fourth food identification method. This technique is biased, since it overestimates the composition of large-bodied prey in the diet. Raptors often swallow small prey whole or with minimal plucking, so the percentage of small-bodied prey is underrepresented at plucking perches.

Examining regurgitated pellets is the fifth technique and has proven to be a very valuable method for determining raptor food habits. When raptors eat prey, they swallow fur, feathers, teeth, bones, and claws along with the meat. These indigestible items are later regurgitated in the form of a firm pellet that biologists can pick apart to identify prey items. Hair fragments from the pellet are soaked in a clearing agent, so internal as well as external hair characteristics can be seen with a microscope. The species of mammalian prey can then be identified using a hair key. Feather fragments in pellets can also be identified by close examination. Although most of these techniques have been used by biologists to learn more about Prairie Falcon food habits, direct observation of prey delivered to eyries and examination of regurgitated pellets are the two methods that have proved particularly valuable.

The Size of Prairie Falcon Prey

Prairie Falcons are fearless predators, capable of killing very large prey. They can kill White-faced Ibis (519 grams), although ibis remains were not located in Prairie Falcon eyries, suggesting the prey was too large for falcons to carry. However, adult Chukars and California Ground Squirrels weighing 500–565 grams were found in eyries and were probably carried by female falcons. Prey of this weight may represent the upper limit that Prairie Falcons can carry. R. M. Bond even reported a half-eaten bobcat kitten on a ledge approximately 10 meters from a falcon eyrie. It was unclear if the falcons killed the 1-kilogram kitten when defending their eyrie, but extensive exploration of the cliff revealed no signs of other large raptors in the area.

Murray Gillespie watched a Prairie Falcon pursue a Canada Goose. Approximately one-half hour after sunset, he heard the goose call before the falcon struck it in the air. The two birds then flew over a stubblefield. The goose tried evasive tactics, such as turning and side-slipping, but the falcon remained close and was able to make two additional passes before the goose landed close to some hay. The falcon landed on a large bale of hay nearby. For nearly ten minutes, the falcon sat on the bale while the agitated goose called continually. Finally, the goose flew away and landed near some hunter's decoys, where it was shot. At that point, the falcon flew off and attacked some ducks, causing them to flush. Several ducks were shot by hunters. The falcon swooped low over a duck that fell in the water as though it was going to try to pick it up, but the hunters' shouts caused the bird to fly away.

Although observations of Prairie Falcons killing large prey are fascinating, small-bodied prey are the key to the falcon's daily survival. The average size prey taken by Prairie Falcons in southwestern Idaho was 97 grams, compared to the average male and female falcon weights of 554 grams and 863 grams, respectively. Douglas Boyce, who studied Prairie Falcons nesting in the Mojave Desert, found that 84 percent of prey items weighed less than 150 grams, or approximately 20 percent of the male falcon's weight. The average weight of food items was 107 grams. He found that for five species of falcons, most prey weighed approximately 20 percent of the male's body weight. Only male falcons were considered because they are the primary providers during nesting. Thus, small rather than large-sized prey primarily affect the movements, survival, and reproductive success of Prairie Falcons.

IV

ECOLOGICAL INTERACTIONS

A. C. Bent describes the Prairie Falcon as a moody creature, a bird of extremes. According to Bent, one never knows what to

Immature Prairie Falcon with meadowlark prey. *Photo by Rick Kline*

expect from this handsome falcon because the expected seldom happens. The bird can dazzle with a burst of speed as it defends its eyrie, or it can look like the picture of listless dejection as it sits stoop-shouldered and motionless for long hours.

Many people have reported various interactions between Prairie Falcons and other birds. When competing for food or a nest site, Prairie Falcons can be very aggressive toward other birds or animals, especially when they seek nest sites from Ravens, owls, and other hawks. On the other hand, Peregrine Falcons and owls can be the aggressors as they displace Prairie Falcons from food or nest-site resources. In some cases, Prairie Falcons seem to have symbiotic relationships with Ravens. But more likely, Ravens nest on the same cliff as Prairie Falcons in order to rob the falcons' food cache.

Prairie Falcons as Neighbors

Prairie Falcons are predators, and most of their interactions relate to the capture of prey. But some behaviors appear to simply be a form of harassment whereby Prairie Falcons choose to torment or even play with other animals. Sometimes mutualistic interactions do occur, as when the Prairie Falcon and another species of animal work together to benefit each other.

The distance Prairie Falcons nest from other raptors is quite variable, depending on the visual isolation of nests and perch sites and food availability. Although Prairie Falcons and Great Horned Owls are natural enemies, they will nest within 30 meters of each other. Common Barn Owls have nested within 5 meters of Prairie Falcons on cliffs in Colorado. When people approach eyries, they may inadvertently flush an owl. Jim Enderson accidentally flushed a Great Horned Owl as he approached an eyrie. Both falcons struck and quickly killed the owl. In another case, a Barn Owl was flushed near a Prairie Falcon eyrie. The female falcon broke the wing of the female owl while the male falcon struck and killed the male owl outright. We accidentally flushed a Barn Owl near a Prairie Falcon eyrie. The female falcon stooped from 35 meters directly overhead and struck the owl in the back and neck, killing it instantaneously. It was later found that the owl's heart had been punctured from the attack. Although the female owl was killed, the young Barn Owl fledglings survived and were raised by the male. These observations suggested that although Prairie Falcons and other raptors may nest in close proximity to one another, human intrusion can disrupt the delicate balance that has been established between neighbors.

Prairie Falcons frequently harass shorebirds. Doug Boyce watched falcons harass Dunlins, Least Sandpipers, and Western Sandpipers that were flying along waterways. One falcon continually flew low over a Lesser Yellowlegs, causing it to repeatedly dive under water to avoid being struck. The falcon continued its harassment for some time until it finally left the area.

A. C. Bent believed that Prairie Falcons delighted in annoying Great Blue Herons. The falcons constantly swooped down toward them, coming very close to their heads. The heron usually ducked as the falcon flew by. In some cases, the herons were also attacked when flying, although he never actually saw one struck. Other people have reported Prairie Falcons harassing waterfowl. Sometimes it appears that Prairie Falcons are simply venting their aggression on nearby birds. Other times, they may harass birds until one panics and becomes easy prey.

Prairie Falcons and Peregrine Falcons

There are examples in the literature that describe interactions between Prairie and Peregrine Falcons. For example, in San Jose, California, a male American Kestrel was caught in a falcon trap, called a noose carpet, that was set on a post. A Gyrfalcon in juvenile plumage began diving on the kestrel. At the same time, a juvenile Peregrine Falcon attacked the Gyrfalcon. Meanwhile, a male Prairie Falcon circled overhead, apparently evaluating the best time to enter the fray. Before he could join in, the Peregrine was struck and killed by an airplane that was landing on the San Jose Airport runway.

During another encounter, a Prairie Falcon apparently flew too close to a Peregrine's eyrie. The female Peregrine, seeking to gain an advantage, circled high above the Prairie before diving at the intruder. The Prairie Falcon rolled onto its back with legs extended. The Prairie Falcon continued to roll over in midflight, greeting each Peregrine attack with open talons. Both birds vocalized during the attacks, producing wailing screams during contact. Physical contact between the birds occurred four times during a seventeen-minute period. The Peregrine pursued the Prairie Falcon eastward after each attack, only to have the Prairie Falcon turn and follow it back to its nest. Neither falcon appeared to have an advantage in flight capabilities.

As the Prairie Falcon approached the female Peregrine for a fifth time, an undetected male Peregrine swooped with closed wings from above and struck the Prairie Falcon before it could roll over and defend itself. The Prairie Falcon fell approximately 250 meters into the canyon, dead. The male Peregrine soared briefly over its nest area before flying out of view. Meanwhile, the female landed exhausted in a nearby tree. Although this encounter shows that the Peregrine can prove superior in some battles, most reported aggressive behaviors between raptors do not result in death.

An unusual relationship existed between a family of Peregrines and a family of Prairies, as reported by David Ellis and David Groat. Both pairs were nesting about 200 meters apart and had a series of hostile encounters. In one encounter, a recently fledged Prairie Falcon entered the Peregrine eyrie and helped itself to some food. After delivering more prey to the eyrie, the female Peregrine Falcon saw the intruder and left the ledge, calling repeatedly as she swooped back and forth. Finally, she landed again and stuck her foot into the narrow pothole, either to push the prey in or to jab at the newcomer. She left, vocalizing and swooping about the eyrie entrance before perching nearby. The juvenile Prairie Falcon appeared at the entrance from time to time but would retreat inside to continue feeding.

None of this activity seemed to concern the resident Peregrine juveniles. Eventually, the female made less noise, and she regained her composure. She called for food occasionally before flying off to forage. Soon the male returned to the eyrie with prey. The young Prairie Falcon quickly snatched the prey before scurrying back, deep into the eyrie. The male hesitated for a moment, then flew out, vocalizing and swooping repeatedly at the eyrie's opening before leaving.

Both Prairie and Peregrine youngsters continued to feed and later were seen sitting side by side with full crops. The parents returned several times and appeared irritated at the young Prairie Falcon but never enough to seriously attempt to oust the youngster. The Prairie Falcon eventually left the eyrie but not the area. Later it was seen nearly colliding with the adult male Peregrine before it landed nearby. After almost two minutes, a second Peregrine Falcon appeared. Both adults repeatedly swooped, attempting to dislodge the Prairie Falcon, but they never harmed it. These observations show that, at times, Prairie Falcon and Peregrine Falcon can co-exist, even with their eyries in close proximity.

Prairie Falcons may have replaced Peregrine Falcons at many nest sites throughout the West, but the decline in Peregrine populations was due primarily to pesticides and habitat loss rather than competitive interactions with Prairie Falcons. In some parts of the country, Peregrines may be increasing at the expense of Prairie Falcons, yet in all likelihood, population shifts are the result of other factors rather than competitive interactions.

Predators of Prairie Falcons

Prairie Falcons have few predators. Animals that venture too close to their eyries are met with the swooping attack of an adult bird. Such attacks have been reported on coyotes, mountain lions, badgers, and a variety of birds. Most of these attacks were to drive intruders from the falcon's immediate nest area.

As we mentioned earlier, Peregrine Falcons do attack Prairie Falcons. Similarly, Golden Eagles and Great Horned Owls do attack and kill Prairie Falcons, but actual harm to Prairie Falcon populations is difficult to document. It is important to remember that nesting Prairie Falcons, Golden Eagles, and Peregrine Falcons have successfully raised young when their nests have been only a few hundred meters apart.

We have watched flocks of blackbirds and other birds mob or harass roosting Prairie Falcons. Although there are no reports of injury, Prairie Falcons try to maneuver away from the attacking birds when in flight. They seem very pestered when blackbirds scold and fly at them but seldom take aggressive action.

Prairie Falcons usually nest at cliffs that offer protection from predators. Snakes, skunks, and other animals crawl into accessible eyries and harm eggs or young birds. Birds that nest on the ledges or caverns of rock cliffs are better protected than those that nest on an accessible ledge.

Young birds learning to fly may be attacked by predators such as the Great Horned Owl or other raptors during the first few days of flight. Again, it is often difficult to accurately document this type of activity, for human intrusion may be the factor that upsets an existing balance.

Although predation appears to be an uncommon cause of mortality for most Prairie Falcons, disease can be an important mortality factor. A number of viruses have been reported in Prairie Falcons that have either died or have showed symptoms of infection when captured. A herpes virus was identified in the cells of the liver, spleen, bone marrow, and small intestines of Prairie Falcons found dead in South Dakota. When falconers take birds into captivity, they are often found to have various types of viral diseases.

External parasites are common on Prairie Falcons. For example, Canadian birds nesting near bats carried a number of tick species. In some cases, ticks became so numerous on adult and young falcons that they sucked enough blood to kill the birds. Ticks may also serve as a vector for other diseases, such as encephalitis and rabies. There is little documentation as to whether these diseases are truly contracted by Prairie Falcons.

In New Mexico, Steve Platt reports the abandonment of one clutch of Prairie Falcon eggs and the death of seven nestlings from two clutches as a result of the Mexican chicken bug. Like ticks, these bugs suck blood from their hosts. Platt counted as many as thirty parasite bugs attached near the eyes and at the base of the legs and wings of a week-old Prairie Falcon.

Nematodes (parasitic worms) have been found in the air sacs of Prairie Falcons. One adult Prairie was taken captive to treat a damaged wing but refused to eat after the wing was set. It died a few days later. Necropsy revealed coiled nematodes packed so tightly in the air sac that they may have actually influenced respiration. Nematodes are fairly common in the air sacs of falcons and apparently cause free-ranging falcons to die from respiratory failure. The stress associated with taking falcons from the wild has caused birds to stop eating and die. Prairie Falcons, like other raptors, have fungi and bacteria growing in their respiratory tracts. In most cases, bacterial and fungal infections do not seem to harm them in the wild, but stress associated with captivity or starvation can lower a falcon's body condition, causing it to succumb to these infections.

Sources

I. THE BIRD

The Bird: Holthuijzen and Eastland 1985.
Vocalization: Tyler 1923.
Size: Holthuijzen and Eastland 1985.
Body Size and Life History: Newton 1979; Cade 1982.
Why Are Female Raptors Typically Larger Than Males?: Darwin 1871; Newton 1979; Amadon 1975; Mueller and Meyer 1985; Ydenberg and Forbes 1991.

II. DISTRIBUTION AND NESTING SITES

Breeding Distribution: A.O.U. 1983; Lanning and Hitchcock 1991.
Nesting Density: Newton 1979; Cade 1982; Oakleaf 1985; Platt 1975; Allen 1987; Garrett and Mitchell 1973; Boyce Jr., Garret, and Walton 1986; Ogden 1975; Ogden and Hornocker 1977; Craig and Craig 1984; U.S.D.I.–B.L.M. 1979; Runde 1987.
Nesting in Trees: Enderson 1964; Runde and Anderson 1986; Goss 1991; Williams and Matteson Jr. 1947; McLaren, Runde and Anderson 1984; Cade 1982.
Occupancy and Nest-Site Fidelity: Newton 1979; Bailey and Niedrach 1933; Ogden and Hornocker 1977; Runde 1987; Squires, Anderson and Oakleaf 1993; Cave 1968; Cade 1982; Haak 1982.
Territoriality: Squires 1986; Squires, Anderson, and Oakleaf 1993; Haak 1982; Ogden and Hornocker 1977; Sitter 1983; DiDonato 1992; Harmata, Durr, and Geduldig 1978; Beebe 1960.
Home Ranges: Haak 1982; Sitter 1983; Harmata, Durr, and Geduldig 1978; Beauvais, Enderson, and Magro 1992; Enderson 1964.

III. HUNTING AND FOOD HABITS

Equipped for Hunting: Cade 1982; Johnsgard 1990; Hoskings and Hoskings 1987.

Hunting Techniques: Cramp and Simmons 1980; Haak 1982; Dekker 1982; White 1962; Merchant 1982; Enderson 1964; Squires, Anderson, and Oakleaf 1989; Holthuijzen, Duley, Hager, Smith, and Wood 1987; Richards 1965; Skinner 1938; Webster Jr. 1944; Thompson and Tabor 1981; Holthuijzen 1990; Cade 1982.

What Do Prairie Falcons Eat?: Haak 1982; Becker 1979; Bent 1937; Boyce Jr. 1985; Denton 1975; Enderson 1964; Holthuijzen 1990; Leedy 1972; MacLaren, Anderson, and Runde 1988; Marti and Braun 1975; Ogden 1973; Porter and White 1973; Smith and Murphy 1973; Squires, Anderson, and Oakleaf 1989; Sherrod 1978; Bent 1937; Beauvais, Enderson, and Margro 1992; Krapu and Swanson 1975; Beasom and Patte 1978; Ankney and Scott 1980; Holthuijzen, Duley, Hager, Smith, and Wood 1987; Steenhof and Kochert 1988.

How Do Biologists Know What Falcons Eat?: Sherrod 1978; Fisher 1883; Moore, Spence, and Dugnolle 1974.

The Size of Prairie Falcon Prey: Porter and White 1973; Bond 1936; Gillespie 1981; Steenhof and Kochert 1988; Boyce Jr. 1985; Cade 1982.

IV. ECOLOGICAL INTERACTIONS

Ecological Interactions: Bent 1937.

Prairie Falcons as Predators: Enderson 1963; Enderson 1964; Bond 1936; Anderson 1988; Boyce Jr. 1985; Bent 1937.

Prairie Falcons and Peregrine Falcons: Balygooyen 1988; Walton 1977; Ellis and Groat 1982; Enderson 1964; Hickey 1942; Porter and White 1973.

Predators of Prairie Falcons: Bent 1937; Enderson 1963.

Prairie Falcons through the Seasons

I

SPRING ARRIVAL

As cold winds rip across the sage grasslands of the western United States and hibernating ground squirrels huddle secure in their burrows, Prairie Falcons already soar high above cliffs, laying claim to their eyries. The lengthening spring days signal to these falcons the beginning of the nesting season. After surviving winter's rigors, Prairie Falcons will now direct their energy to the arduous task of raising young.

Spring Arrival on Nesting Territories

Prairie Falcons often lay claim to their nesting territories long before falcon enthusiasts brave the cold spring weather of western prairies. In fact, in Utah, adult falcons may remain in the vicinity of their eyries throughout the winter. Canadian birds have also been seen perching on nest cliffs throughout the winter and into the spring. However, most Prairie Falcons migrate from their nesting territories in order to winter in better foraging areas.

The date Prairie Falcons return to their eyries in the spring varies with location. In Idaho, Prairie Falcons nesting in the Snake River Birds of Prey National Conservation Area have been seen flying about their nesting cliffs in February, after having been absent all winter. Prairie Falcons nesting in Colorado and Wyoming do not return to their eyries until mid-March; in western Montana, some falcons are not paired until April.

Prairie Falcon pairs that nest together are believed to winter in separate wintering areas. In the spring, either the male or female falcon may be the first to return to the eyrie. It seems to vary with different individuals and locations. For example, in Oregon, male Prairie Falcons were the first to return to the eyrie in the spring. However, in Colorado, nine of eleven first arrivals were females. The pair member that first returns to the eyrie probably depends on that bird's pairing status, age, and wintering locale.

Courtship

Courtship behaviors of many birds involve bizarre dances, stupendous flights, odd vocalizations, and fierce battles over territories and mates. However, many courtship behaviors that are depicted in the literature for Prairie Falcons may simply describe different pairs fighting over the same nest cliff. Since male and female Prairie Falcons usually do not associate with one another during the winter, pair bonding occurs at nest sites. For some pairs, preliminary breeding behaviors are limited to mutual soaring or patrolling along the cliff face. Falcons also may simply sit on conspicuous perches as a means of claiming their nest site. Other Prairie Falcon pairs engage in more elaborate courtship behaviors.

Female Prairie Falcons are more aggressive than females of other falcon species, and this aggression is a distinguishing characteristic of their behavior. Females may overtly attack males during early courtship. As a consequence, head-low bow displays (see Figure 2) and other appeasement displays occur frequently and occupy a greater proportion of courtship time compared to other falcons. Female dominance may be very important in enforcing the division of labor that is common among falcons; it ensures the male's role as the primary food provider. Males are also aggressive, and both pair members can inflict serious injury to each other during courtship. Thus, falcons have evolved a behavioral repertoire that communicates the mood and motivation of each pair member. This allows falcons, heavily armed with sharp beaks and talons, to interact with their mates without harming one another.

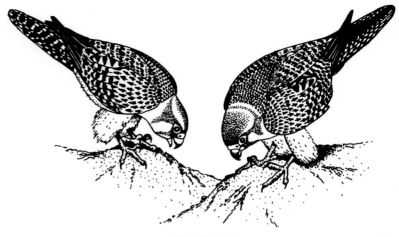

FIGURE 2
Head-low bow display during Prairie Falcon courtship.
After Cade 1982.

PRELIMINARY COURTSHIP BEHAVIORS

Selecting the nest ledge is one of the earliest courtship activities
of Prairie Falcons. Typically, the male falcon goes to the ledge
first, followed shortly by the female. On the ledge, they turn in
small circles, head down and side-by-side, while making *chup-
ping* sounds. Sometimes one bird will try to put its head between the legs of the other bird, attempting to knock its mate
off its feet. Although the birds may repeat this behavior over
and over again, it is rarely seen because it occurs for only a short
period of time, often only a day or two.

Peter Wrege and Tom Cade describe a similar early-courtship
display that most falcons use, including Prairie Falcons. During
the head-low bow display, falcons hold their head below the
body plane, their beak directed away from the mate, usually toward the eyrie floor, with their feathers sleeked down. Falcons
often bow vigorously during this display. Pair members will use
this display when they are close to each other. Its purpose
seems to be to communicate passive intentions between pair
members.

NEST LEDGE DISPLAYS

Males initially visit many ledges, busily scraping and examining potential eyries while paying little attention to the female. After choosing a ledge, males try to attract females to the ledge through calls and displays. During male ledge displays, the male approaches the scrape (a depression that is often dug into the sand on nest ledges) and assumes a horizontal, head-low posture while making an *eechip* vocalization. When sexual motivation is particularly high, males will add a "high-step" or "tippy-toe" gait, producing a side-to-side swagger. After five or ten seconds, the male will pause and look at the female, checking her response. Sometimes males will also fly repeatedly to and from the ledge to attract attention. At other times, males may simply stand at the ledge making a *chups* vocalization while looking at the female.

Females also have ledge displays, but they are less intense than the males' and are often difficult to distinguish from simple ledge-sitting. Typically, a female holds her head, body, and tail horizontal as she approaches the scrape while giving an *eechip* vocalization. Often, a female will turn around and around on the nest ledge while scraping a depression in the sand. She rarely pauses to look at the male.

Mutual ledge displays occur when both pair members are on the nest ledge (see Figure 3). Ledge displays are most intense when both the male and the female falcon are at the eyrie. Each bird assumes a horizontal position while holding its beak close to the eyrie floor. At the same time, each calls *eechip* vigorously. "Billing" is a display that is often seen during mutual ledge displays or on other occasions when pair members are in close proximity. Billing involves both pair members twisting their heads sideways and nibbling between beaks. The female often holds her head lower and looks up while the male looks down.

COURTSHIP FEEDING

Male Prairie Falcons also use food to attract female attention. The male will try to coax the female to the nest ledge with

FIGURE 3
Feeding display during Prairie Falcon courtship. After Cade 1982.

food; he will then fly away, leaving her perched at the ledge. Males resort to courtship feeding as a means of strengthening the pair bond.

Like many raptors, male Prairie Falcons chiefly provide food for the brood while females defend the nest site. When a male flies into the immediate nest area with food, the female wails in a loud call that can be heard up to a kilometer from the eyrie. A female Prairie Falcon is not polite when taking food from the male. She often flies or runs over to the perched male and rips the food from his talons while calling and beating her wings incessantly.

Food-transfer displays involve transferring food from one mate to the other, usually from male to female. If the male does not have food, the female uses a "wail" call combined with a vertical head-low posture to solicit a food transfer. When prey is secured, the male will hold up a prey item in his beak, standing vertically with his head up, while the female maintains a head-low posture; both sexes give *eechip* vocalizations during food transfers.

As courtship proceeds, the female begins to go to the nest ledge on her own. She busies herself by scraping a depression in the sand on the eyrie floor that will eventually contain the eggs, or she may simply perch beside the ledge. Frequently, females wail constantly, begging the male for food or soliciting copulations.

Male Prairie Falcons begin copulating with females anywhere from several days to a month before egg-laying. Copulations usually occur immediately after the male feeds the female. The birds exhibit a hitched-wing display (see Figure 4) prior to copulations. While both sexes engage in hitched-wing displays, they are usually male displays used to communicate an intent to copulate. During hitched-wing flight displays, the wings are held high with short wing-beats, mainly from the wrist. The males keep their legs forward and tails depressed, resulting in a slow-motion, bouncing flight. They fly in this manner to and from copulations and during precopulatory behaviors. Males may also exhibit a hitched-wing display while standing. They briefly (for two seconds) hold their heads low and their wings up high against their bodies, forming a deep V-shaped depression along the back.

Females communicate their willingness to copulate through copulation-solicitation displays. They begin soliciting males with vocalizations while assuming a head-low bow. This is usually done when the male is at a distance. If the male shows an interest in the display, the female assumes a horizontal head-low posture. She calls often, holds her tail horizontal, and raises her panel feathers as she orients herself perpendicular to the male. This display lasts for approximately thirty seconds. As the male shows his intention to mount, she sleeks her panel feathers, crouches, and leans forward, moving her tail to the side to prepare for copulation.

FIGURE 4
Hitched-wing display during Prairie Falcon courtship.
After Cade 1982.

During copulation, the female bends forward approximately 45° and gives a copulation wail (see Figure 5). As the male mounts, the female spreads her wings about one-fourth open. She holds her tail up and to the side. During copulation, the male flaps his wings constantly in order to balance when mounting the female. He makes a *chitter* vocalization during copulations as he presses his cloaca against the female's. Rapid wing beats accompany his cloacal press. After only a few seconds, the male finishes copulating and departs with a hitched-wing display.

Females usually begin soliciting copulations about three weeks before laying. Two to three weeks before egg laying, copulations are frequent—two or three copulations per hour. Each copulation lasts eight to ten seconds. One week before laying, the number of copulations increases to three or four per hour.

In southwestern Idaho, a total of fifty-two pairs of Prairie

FIGURE 5
Copulation of Prairie Falcons. After Cade 1982.

Falcons were observed for 613 days. The total number of copulations during the pre-incubation period (51 days) was 194 copulations per clutch, or an average of 3.8 copulations per day.
Prairie Falcons copulate at a high rate compared to Ospreys (59
copulations/clutch) and Merlins (42 copulations/clutch), but
at a lower rate compared to Northern Goshawks (500 copula-
tions/clutch), and American Kestrels (690 copulations). Birds
of prey copulate more frequently than other birds. The purpose
of these frequent copulations may be to dilute the sperm of
possible competitors or to strengthen pair bonds.

Just prior to egg laying, female Prairie Falcons become le-
thargic or "dumpy." They sit quietly near the nest ledge with
feathers puffed out, reluctant to fly or defend their eyrie from
intruders. However, they become their old irascible selves when

the first egg is laid, and their aggression increases throughout egg laying.

Prairie Falcon courtship usually follows a sequence of behaviors, but the behaviors are not always in the order we describe. For example, courtship feeding, nest scraping, and mating can all happen on the same day. In addition, courtship may be very short in duration. Richard Fyfe has observed that an individual Prairie Falcon may remain at a cliff for a week or more before its mate arrives; the pair may then copulate the same day with little, if any, preliminary courtship. This may occur when pairs have long-established pair bonds.

Seasonal Timing of Nesting

Food abundance is one very important factor that affects when Prairie Falcons nest. For example, Townsend's Ground Squirrels compose approximately 40–80 percent of the diet for Prairie Falcons nesting in the Snake River Birds of Prey National Conservation Area. There, the falcons' entire nesting schedule is tied to the squirrels' life-cycle. Prairie Falcons arrive on their territories in January, just as ground squirrels begin emerging from their winter dormancy. Prairie Falcons then lay their eggs, just as juvenile squirrels become active above ground. The young falcons hatch when squirrel densities are highest and parent birds are best able to provide adequate food to the hungry brood. The young falcons fledge and leave their eyries in July, just as the ground squirrels gradually disappear underground to begin estivation (a state of dormancy or torpor during late summer). The fledglings then migrate to higher elevations to exploit new prey sources. Thus, the entire nesting rhythm of this falcon population is inextricably linked to its prey.

Latitude and elevation also influence when Prairie Falcons begin nesting. Richard Williams studied how latitude and elevation both affect the dates when eggs are laid. The eyries he observed ranged from 25.5° to 54° N in latitude and from sea level to 3,688 meters in elevation. Williams found that 64 percent of the variation in laying dates could be attributed to differences in latitude, while 21 percent could be explained by differences in elevation. In other words, falcons nest later the farther they are north and the higher the elevation. The lowest nest sites in Williams' study (below 700 meters) were at the highest latitudes (52° N, Canada), and the nest sites at the highest elevations (2,800 meters) were associated with the southernmost latitudes (25° N, Mexico). The northernmost Canadian falcons selected low elevation sites with more equitable climates, whereas the southernmost birds selected the cool mountaintops of Mexico.

Since such factors as prey abundance, latitude, and elevation all affect when Prairie Falcons nest, different falcon populations have different nesting schedules. In northern California, Prairie Falcons usually court in March and lay their clutch by 14 April. The eggs hatch by 15 May (n=23), and the young fledge by 22 June. In New Mexico, Prairie Falcons lay eggs from 4 to 30 April. Eggs hatch from 4 to 30 May, and young birds fledge from 7 June to 3 July. In Oregon, Prairie Falcons begin incubation on 1 April and the eggs usually hatch by 16 May. Young birds usually fledge by 24 June. In northern Mexico, Prairie Falcons may fledge as early as 20 May through 23 June.

Nesting

INCUBATION

Female Prairie Falcons are primarily responsible for incubation, which lasts 29–33 days. Biologists often assume that if five nestlings in a clutch are all similarly aged, the female must have delayed incubation until the last egg was laid, thus helping to synchronize the hatch. However, recent studies show that incubation begins gradually. For example, one Prairie Falcon pair incubated 15, 22, 64, and 90 percent of daylight hours for the first four days after laying the first egg. The female was on the nest at dusk and dawn on five of six occasions, suggesting that

Prairie Falcons cover their eggs at night even before steady incubation begins.

During incubation, females pass the time by intermittent dozing and egg turning. Egg turning is accomplished with a special action. First, the parent rises up and peers at the eggs. She then sweeps her bill gently between the eggs toward her belly. This shifts the eggs' position one to the other. Turning ensures that the eggs' internal membranes do not stick together and that heat is distributed evenly. When walking near the eggs, parents hold their feet in a special position, with the hind toe forward between the front toes and the front toes clutched together with claws pointing inward. This prevents the falcon from accidentally spiking the eggs.

Prairie Falcon eggs are smaller than those of Peregrine Falcons and are approximately the size of a small chicken egg. They average 52.3 × 40.5 millimeters in size. The eggs are nearly oval in shape, with a granulated to smooth surface. Egg coloration is highly variable. Small brown dots and blotches often cover the egg, nearly concealing its background color. These marking are burnt-brownish to cinnamon on a fairly light-colored background. Some eggs lack obvious speckling and are almost entirely cream colored.

CLUTCH SIZE

Prairie Falcon clutches average 4.5 eggs. Clutches of five are most common; clutches of six occur less frequently than clutches of three or four eggs. In southern Alberta, Canada, the average Prairie Falcon clutch size is 4.5 eggs (n=20); 5-egg clutches were the most common (n=11). Average clutch sizes from other populations included 4.56 eggs (n=127), Wyoming; 4.5 eggs (n=55), Colorado and Wyoming; 3.2 eggs, New Mexico; and 4.3 eggs, Idaho.

The maximum Prairie Falcon clutch size is usually six eggs. However, a clutch of seven eggs was found in an eyrie situated atop an abandoned raven nest, but none of these eggs hatched. In North Dakota, an eyrie contained seven eggs plus one hatched young. In this case, it appears the female laid a replacement clutch without removing the initial clutch, so the eight eggs did not represent a single clutch.

RENESTING

When raptors fail in their first nesting attempt, they often try again by laying a second clutch. This is especially true if the first clutch is destroyed early in the nesting season. Biologists use this ability of falcons to lay a second clutch to reestablish Peregrine Falcon populations. They remove the eggs from the first clutch as soon as they are laid and hatch them in an incubator while the falcons produce a second clutch that they raise themselves. This procedure doubles the productivity of this endangered species. The recycling time—the time from initial egg loss until the second clutch is laid—is approximately sixteen days for Prairie Falcons.

The importance of late nesting and renesting for Prairie Falcons is not well understood. Late nesting often suggests the pair has renested. George Allen and others studied fourteen late nesting attempts (hatchings after 12 June) from Prairie Falcon populations nesting in southern Idaho (Snake River Birds of Prey National Conservation Area), northeastern New Mexico, and northeastern Colorado. Only 8 of 517 nesting attempts (1.5 percent) for birds nesting in Idaho had hatch dates of 12 June or later. Two of these were confirmed renesting attempts. That only 1.5 percent of clutches were renesting attempts indicates that Prairie Falcons seldom renest. However, in Alberta, Prairie Falcons replaced four of five failed clutches with a second clutch.

SEVERE SPRING STORMS

On the High Plains of the western United States, severe spring snowstorms can cause Prairie Falcons to abandon their nesting attempts. Sometimes the sand moved by melting snow flows into the nesting scrape and partly buries the eggs. Other times it is unclear how the storm causes nest failure. Possibly, the male falcons are unable to hunt for several days, so the females are less attentive or abandon their nests. A cold spring storm will rapidly chill the eggs of all but the most attentive adults. Nests located on exposed buttes are particularly vulnerable to the effects of spring storms.

In north-central Wyoming, we observed firsthand the devastating effects spring snowstorms can have on nesting Prairie Falcons. From 25–27 April 1984, a strong spring storm dumped approximately 64 centimeters of snow on our study area. The ground was covered with at least 20 centimeters of snow for ten days. We were unable to reach our study area because of road closures, but ranchers said the storm killed more than 50 percent of their sheep and 25 percent of their cattle. One rancher told us that the "spaces between his stacked hay bales were packed with dead sparrows." Apparently, these small birds died of exposure even though they were huddled between hay bales.

All five pairs of Prairie Falcons in our study area quit nesting after this storm. Four of the five pairs laid eggs following the storm, but only one clutch hatched. These nestlings died almost immediately. Therefore, no young were produced in 1984, compared to this population's usual production of sixteen fledglings (based on a three-year average). The falcon pairs failed regardless of where their nests were oriented on the nest buttes. In 1985, the usual number of nestlings were produced, suggesting the storm's effect was short-lived.

We wanted to understand why our birds failed, so we sampled birds and small mammals to determine how the falcons' food supply was affected by the storm. We discovered that while more prey-sized birds were present in our study area in 1985 than in 1984 (the year of the storm), small mammal populations were unaffected. Since ground squirrels may delay spring emergence during snowstorms, it is possible that the falcons in our study area depended entirely on avian prey whose numbers were reduced by the storms. Jim Enderson observed that after an early March snowstorm, Horned Larks were no longer present near falcon nest sites, and all nest sites were subsequently abandoned. We believe the falcons in our study area also failed when songbirds were no longer an abundant food source.

EGG MORTALITY

Not all eggs that Prairie Falcons lay will hatch. Some eggs are infertile or get eaten by predators; others simply disappear, and no one knows their fate. Eighty-one cases of lost eggs were documented for Prairie Falcons in Idaho: 30 percent of the eggs were lost to infertility; 23 percent to predation; 23 percent disappeared; 12 percent were accidentally broken, probably by activities of the parents; 6 percent had dead, undeveloped embryos; and 6 percent contained dead embryos that were well developed. Predation mostly occurs at eyries that are accessible to mammalian predators.

I I
THE SUMMER

In the early summer, adult Prairie Falcons are responsible for feeding and defending their recently hatched young. Like most raptors, male Prairie Falcons primarily provide food for the clutch, whereas females defend and care for their young. However, the amount of time female Prairie Falcons spend at their eyries varies according to the age of the nestlings, the weather, the male's behavior, and the attentiveness of the individual female. For example, early in the nesting cycle, females may spend 98 percent of their time at the nest, but by fledging, this may have decreased to as little as 3 percent. Prairie Falcons, just like humans, display different parenting styles. We have seen some females remain at their eyries until the young fledge, while others hunt extensively and actively provide food for their nestlings.

Productivity

During early summer, Prairie Falcons expend nearly all their energy into raising young. The number of nestlings they produce is affected by several factors, including the female's body condition, the weather, and human disturbance. As mentioned earlier, one of the most important elements affecting productivity is prey abundance. Changes in ground-squirrel densities can account for more than 98 percent of the year-to-year variation in the number of nestlings that are produced. In Idaho, ground-squirrel densities were high in 1975 and 1976, but a severe winter drought reduced their population level. By March 1978, squirrel density was only 25 percent of pre-drought levels. As prey declined, Prairie Falcons switched to alternate prey, such as pigeons and jackrabbits, but their productivity still plummeted. In 1978, only 289 young falcons were fledged, compared to 526 and 631 fledglings produced in 1975 and 1976, respectively. Prairie Falcons did not lay smaller clutches when prey was scarce. Instead, the nestlings they did produce suffered high mortality.

Biologists use a range of parameters to characterize the productivity of most Prairie Falcon populations. Before the health of a population can be determined, biologists need to know the occupancy rate, or the number of known eyries that have birds present during a given year (Table 1); the success rate, or the percentage of nesting pairs that successfully raise at least one fledgling (Table 3); and the productivity rate, or the number of hatchlings that survive to fledging (Table 4). Based on these parameters, biologists estimate that for the population to persist, Prairie Falcons must produce an average of 1.71 to 2.00 young per occupied site. If these measures indicate the falcon population is declining, appropriate management actions must be initiated to ensure the population's survival.

Young Nestlings

Female Prairie Falcons become very reluctant to leave their eyries when the eggs are ready to hatch, even to defend the territory from intruders or to get food from the male. Chicks begin pipping about 24–48 hours before they hatch. They can be

TABLE 3

Nesting Success of Prairie Falcon Populations, 1960–1985

STUDY AREA AND DURATION	% SUC-CESSFUL NESTS [a,b]	SOURCE
Alberta–Saskatchewan, 1966–1968	71	Fyfe et al. 1969
Alberta, 1967–1971	88	Edwards 1973
Saskatchewan, 1973–1974	71	Oliphant et al. 1976
Colorado–Wyoming, 1960–1962	41	Enderson 1962
Colorado, 1969–1970	72	Grater 1970
Idaho, 1970–1972	83	Ogden 1975
Idaho, 1975–1978	73	U.S.B.L.M. 1979
Montana, 1970–1971	66	Leedy 1972
Oregon, 1973–1974	84	Denton 1975
Wyoming, 1980–1985	66	Platt unpubl. data
Wyoming, 1982–1984	74	MacLarren unpubl. data
Wyoming, 1982–1985	50	Squires 1986
Unweighted mean	70	

Source: Runde 1987.

[a] Percentage of occupied territories, or pairs producing young.

[b] Ninety-five percent confidence interval is 61–79%.

heard tapping and cheeping inside the eggs even earlier. For a few hours after hatching, young Prairie Falcons are too exhausted even to raise their heads. Soon, the mother falcon's warmth and the warm prairie winds dry their down. The young chicks look like a pile of loose cotton as they huddle together

TABLE 4

Reproductive Success of Prairie Falcon Populations, 1960–1985

STUDY AREA AND DURATION	PRODUCTIVITY[a,b]	SOURCE
Alberta–Saskatchewan, 1966–1968	2.53	Fyfe et al. 1969
Alberta, 1967–1971	2.50	Edwards 1973
Saskatchewan, 1973–1974	2.84	Oliphant et al. 1976
Colorado–Wyoming, 1960–1962	1.90	Enderson 1962
Colorado, 1969–1970	2.86	Grater 1970
Colorado, 1970–1972	3.41	Oledorff and Stoddart 1974
Colorado, 1976–1978	2.51	Platt 1981
California, 1969–1972	1.59	Garrett and Mitchell 1973
California, 1974–1978	1.87	Walton 1977, Platt 1981
Idaho, 1970–1972	3.10	Ogden 1975
Idaho, 1975–1978	2.50	U.S.B.L.M. 1979
Montana, 1970–1971	1.90	Leedy 1972
Oregon, 1973–1974	2.49	Denton 1975
Washington, 1971–1972	2.99	Parker 1972 and 1973
Wyoming, 1980–1985	2.18	Platt unpubl. data
Wyoming, 1982–1984	2.62	MacLarren unpubl. data
Wyoming, 1982–1985	1.98	Squires 1986
Unweighted mean	2.46	

Source: Runde 1987.
[a]Mean number of young per occupied territory, or pairs, per year.
[b]Ninety-five percent confidence interval is 2.20–2.71.

Rapelling into falcon eyrie to band nestlings. *Photo by Rick Kline*

to keep warm. The behavioral repertoire of young nestlings is quite limited. They spend up to 80 percent of their time resting and sleeping; otherwise, they are either preening, feeding, or exercising.

Nestlings eat an average of 88 grams of food per day. The number of times the adults must feed the brood depends on the number and size of the young and the prey size. Parents of large broods that feed small-prey items have to feed their young more often than do parents of smaller broods that are fed large items. The number of feedings per day usually varies from three to eight.

In Idaho we observed that during early brood rearing, male Prairie Falcons spent more time near their eyries in years when squirrel abundance was high compared to years when it was low. Apparently, high squirrel abundance allowed males to decrease the time they spent foraging for their brood. Each nestling in Idaho received an average of 1.7 feedings per day.

Nestling Prairie Falcons remain downy until they are about eighteen days old. From days five to seven, nestlings are covered entirely in pure white down with bright pink skin showing through. At this age, the nestlings are only 10 centimeters long and are barely able to lift their heads.

Between nine and eleven days of age, nestlings are still covered with white down, but the spinal apteria (a feather tract) becomes visible. The young are now growing stronger, able to sit up with their heads high. They are about 12 centimeters long.

From days thirteen to fifteen, feather development is beginning to show on their wings, but their bodies are still covered with white down. Primary and secondary feathers are encased in dark gray sheaths that protrude from their wings, which are still covered with natal down. Both spinal and humeral apteria are visible. Nestlings at this age are approximately 18 centimeters long.

Between seventeen and nineteen days of age, the tips of primaries, secondaries, and tail feathers have all begun to burst through feather sheaths. Down covers all areas of bare skin, and juvenile scapular feathers are becoming obvious.

At days twenty-one to twenty-three, the primary coverts (upper wing surface feathering) are out of their sheaths and now contrast with the body down. Feathers are beginning to grow on the side of the nestlings' heads, near the ear openings, and along the back. Nestlings at this age are strong and can run quickly around the eyrie and rip prey. Adults with food are immediately mobbed by the voracious youngsters.

Twenty-five to twenty-seven-day-old nestlings have wings that are 50 percent feathered with distinct scapulars. Their upper tail coverts are beginning to emerge through the down, and dark feathers are conspicuous around the eyes. However, their breasts still remain downy.

By twenty-nine to thirty-one days of age, young Prairie Falcons are almost adultlike. Their heads are 50–75 percent feathered, and their striped breast feathers are obvious, although down still shows on parts of their wings. At this age, young falcons are growing feathers so fast they may actually lose body weight, even though food is usually abundant.

When nestlings are between thirty-three to thirty-five days of age, they are ready to fledge. Their heads and backs are 90–95 percent feathered, as are the tops of their wings. Their legs are now approximately 90 percent feathered.

Young falcons just out of the nest are buffier than adults, with a reddish tinge and more stripes. Their eyes are brown, and their feet and legs are slate-colored. Gradually, the juvenile plumage becomes lighter and more spotted instead of streaked. Their feet and legs turn yellow-white during late summer.

Nestling Mortality

Although most eyries are located on vertical cliff walls that are guarded by fierce parents, some nestling Prairie Falcons die before they fledge. Mortality rates for nestlings are approximately 10–15 percent. Most of these chicks are lost to predation, disease, accidents, or aggressive attacks from neighboring raptors.

Predation can be an especially important mortality factor for nestlings, especially at eyries that lack sheer-wall protection. Of seventeen eyries accessible to mammalian predators in Idaho, eight failed to produce young. One pair of Prairie Falcons abandoned their surviving nestling after its four nest-mates were killed by a bobcat.

Even the most attentive parents cannot prevent ectoparasites from killing nestlings. In New Mexico, most nestling mortalities were caused by an ectoparasite—the Mexican chicken bug.

Young nestlings ready for banding. *Photo by Rick Kline*

Female feeding month-old nestlings. *Photo by Rick Kline*

This parasite caused the abandonment of three falcon eggs (one clutch) and the deaths of seven young. Ectoparasites usually kill young falcons that are between two and four weeks of age. Infestations of swallow bedbugs (*Oeciacus vicarius*) are so bad at some eyries that nestlings fledge prematurely trying to escape, which may cause them to fall to their deaths.

Fledging

Fledging is when the young birds learn to fly, hunt, and avoid enemies. Prairie Falcons fledge from their eyries gradually. Different siblings leave the eyrie at slightly different ages over several days. Nestlings will sometimes roost at the nest ledge the night after their initial departure but soon will venture further afield as they grow stronger. Adult falcons will still feed the youngsters during this period of adjustment, but fledglings must also begin foraging on their own. Anyone who has watched how clumsy these youngsters are when hunting prey realizes how much they must learn in order to develop their parents' elegant hunting style. They do learn quickly, however. Within a week or two they are capable fliers and are ready to strike out on their own.

Fledging is a very tenuous time for young falcons. In Idaho, 50 percent of all nestling mortalities occur during this period. Many deaths result when neighboring adult falcons attack other pairs' fledglings (see "Territoriality" in section II of the previous chapter). Starvation is also an important cause of fledgling mortality.

Young Prairie Falcons disperse from their natal territories at approximately 65 days of age. Usually, females remain near their eyries a few days longer than males. In Idaho, Mary McFadzen and John Marzluff noted that, after fledglings left their natal territory, they stayed for approximately 3–4 days on benchlands near the Snake River Canyon. Often, two or three youngsters grouped together during this period. Staging for a brief period may give fledglings time to develop their hunting skills. Youngsters remained on benchlands for longer periods during years when ground squirrels were abundant compared to low-abundance years. By late July, the recent fledglings had left the study area.

III

FALL AND WINTER DISPERSAL

The life history of young Prairie Falcons after they fledge is not well understood. We know little of their habitat requirements, food habits, movements, or their interactions with parents and other siblings. We do know that the distribution of prey strongly affects their movements. For example, in Idaho, only 4 of 259 color-marked nestlings were observed near their nests after 15 July. The latest sighting was 28 July. No marked falcons were observed within 100 kilometers of their nests from midsummer on, which indicates that these youngsters completely left the area immediately after fledging. Their abandonment of natal territories was attributed to low prey abundance.

For example, Townsend's Ground Squirrels, the principal prey for the Idaho falcons, estivate (sleep underground to escape the heat) by mid-July, so they are unavailable to the fledgling falcons. Young Prairie Falcons apparently move to higher elevations, where prey is more abundant. Two youngsters were seen in high valleys (>1,900 meters) where Richardson's Ground Squirrels were plentiful. Young Prairie Falcons are even common on the alpine tundra, where they hunt pikas during the summer. Sometimes young falcons move long distances after they fledge. Of the marked Idaho fledglings, two falcons moved northeast to Montana, and a third bird was seen in Utah. In mid-September, a young bird was recovered as far away as Coahuila, Mexico.

In June, 1960, Jim Enderson established counting routes on the Laramie plains to study the post-nesting movements of Prairie Falcons. This high intermountain basin (3,300 meters) is bordered by mountains on three sides, all of which exceed 3,400 meters. The greatest number of Prairie Falcons he observed on a single day was eleven on 4 August 1960 and sixteen birds on 28 July 1961. Enderson trapped, tagged, and monitored several of these birds and considered them residents of the post-nesting area if they remained in the area for at least seven days. In 1961, eighteen females and six males were residents. All the birds Enderson banded were adults; juveniles were present only as transients. Most resident birds remained in the post-nesting area for at least thirty-one days before they left in mid-October.

Enderson found no evidence that the same Prairie Falcons returned to the same post-nesting area; none of the previously banded birds was recaptured. He also did not recapture birds that had nested or had fledged from nests in the vicinity of the

Immature Prairie Falcon ready to fledge. *Photo by Rick Kline*

Laramie Plains. Enderson could not determine where the birds that used the post-nesting area near Laramie were from, but apparently they were from other regions. This study also illustrates how little we know about dispersal patterns and post-nesting areas used by Prairie Falcons.

The movements of young falcons after they fledge and those of their parents after nesting are areas of study that need addi-

Two recently fledged Prairie Falcons. *Photo by Rick Kline*

tional research. It is important that we understand these movements, since healthy Prairie Falcon populations may depend on certain habitats during the late summer and early fall that are unknown to biologists responsible for their management.

Prairie Falcons disperse approximately 36.5 kilometers (range 0–225 kilometers) from their natal territory to their first known breeding territory. Female Prairie Falcons disperse farther than males: males disperse approximately 12.9 kilometers (n=33; range 0–132 kilometers), while females move an average 54.4 kilometers (n=55; range 0–225). Other raptors such as European Sparrow Hawks, Merlins, and Peregrine Falcons disperse in a similar manner.

Dispersal from natal territories lessens the chance of inbreeding by reducing the possibility that matings occur with close relations. (This is not absolute, since Doug Runde observed one male and one female nesting in their respective natal territories.) Paul Greenwood found that most animals with resource-defense (i.e., territorial) mating systems have female-biased natal dispersal. The sex that controls the reproductive resource is best able to establish a territory in a familiar area, whereas the opposite sex disperses to locate high-quality territories. Since Prairie Falcon males appear to control breeding sites by selecting nest cliffs, they disperse shorter distances than females.

The distance that Prairie Falcons disperse is not that far, given their mobility. They may nest near their natal territory because a detailed knowledge of prey distribution may be beneficial to falcons, especially for males responsible for feeding their hungry families. Hunting experience from previous years may help males locate prey concentrations within their large hunting areas.

Winter Biology

The winter biology of most raptors, including Prairie Falcons, is difficult to study because individual birds disperse widely as they exploit unpredictable food resources. We do know that the winter range of Prairie Falcons is extensive, extending from their breeding range in southern Canada, south to Mexico, including Baja California, Sonora, Durango, Zacatecas, Aguascalientes, Nuevo Leon, and Tamaulipas. Occasionally, they are even observed as far east as Manitoba, Minnesota, Illinois, Indiana, and Tennessee.

The degree to which raptors migrate during the winter reflects their general ecology. For example, Golden Eagles in Idaho feed on Black-tailed Jackrabbits, which are available year-round, so these birds remain near their territories throughout the year. Red-tailed Hawks have very general diets and easily shift to alternative prey when their primary prey, such as ground squirrels, estivate and are unavailable. In addition, Red-tailed Hawks depend on insects to a greater degree than do eagles or falcons. When the Red-tails' food resources become unavailable by late fall, the birds migrate. Prairie Falcons are fairly restricted in their diet selection and feed on a few species of prey that are seasonally abundant. Therefore, they must migrate in search of abundant prey.

We usually think of birds that migrate in the fall as moving south to warm climates. However, this is not always the case. Jim Enderson summarized band recoveries from 1930 to 1961 (83 nestlings and 9 adults or immatures) and found there was a strong tendency for Prairie Falcons to migrate eastward from the Rocky Mountain states where they nested to the Plains states and provinces during their first winter (see Figure 6). For example, falcons banded in Wyoming and Colorado moved to the northeast, east, or southeast; four of five birds banded in California were later recovered east of the Continental Divide. Prairie Falcons that were banded as nestlings and were not recovered until after their first year had the same eastward migration. A bird banded in California was recovered five years and five months later during the fall in Saskatchewan; a bird banded in Wyoming was recovered fourteen years later, wintering in South Dakota.

Recent research supports Enderson's original conclusion that Prairie Falcons migrate in an east-to-southeasterly direction. Falcons banded in Idaho were recovered in Kansas, Mexico, Arizona, Utah, Montana, and eastern Idaho. More than 50 percent of the recoveries and sightings further than 100 kilometers from their banding locations were east of the Continental

FIGURE 6
Movement pattern of young falcons. After Enderson 1964.

Divide. The winter movements of Prairie Falcons may take them as far as 2,170 kilometers from their nest sites. Apparently, Prairie Falcons move to the eastern plains in search of abundant populations of Horned Larks (see section III, "Hunting and Food Habits," in Chapter One).

How Long Do Prairie Falcons Live?

Adult Prairie Falcons generally live four to five years. Anytime people remove birds from a population, it is helpful to know what "harvest" rate is acceptable without adversely affecting that population. Most animals, including Prairie Falcon populations, produce more young than are needed to replace adults. These excess birds are available to colonize new areas or, in the case of Prairie Falcons, be harvested by falconers. If a population is not producing enough young to replace itself, it will decline, as did Peregrine populations when DDT caused egg-shell thinning. Initially, "surplus" Peregrines likely replaced breeders; however, as surplus birds declined and breeders died out, the overall population plummeted. For a while, the decline was not noticed, but it precipitated over a number of years until suddenly the total Peregrine population disappeared over a large portion of its range.

Recruitment Standard

The average number of young each pair needs to produce per year in order to maintain a stable population is called the recruitment standard. Productivity that falls below the recruitment standard suggests a declining, or potentially declining, population. Conversely, when productivity is greater than the recruitment standard, the population may be producing a "harvestable surplus" of birds. Such ideas assume, however, that the local population is not subject to immigration or emigration, or that the two are equal.

The recruitment standard is affected by the age at which birds first breed. In most Prairie Falcon populations, some birds breed during their first year, but most do not breed until their second year. Therefore, the recruitment standard is somewhere between two and three nestlings. In other words, each pair must produce an average of approximately three young per year if the population is going to remain stable. If falcons fail to be productive for a year—during times of severe weather, for example—they must produce more young on average during the next three to five years in order to maintain a stable population.

In western Wyoming, Douglas Runde studied a population of Prairie Falcons for five years and made follow-up observations for an additional three years. His purpose was to investigate what impact removing young birds would have on population stability.

Runde's study divided the nesting birds into two groups: a treatment group that ranged in size from 20 to 26 pairs of falcons, and a larger control group that contained 40–60 pairs. All known nesting territories were visited twice each summer to determine nest-site occupancy rates and breeding success. Runde artificially reduced the breeding success in the treatment group by removing nestlings from nests. He removed equal numbers of each sex and left at least two youngsters in each eyrie. Nestlings that were taken from treatment nests were placed with foster pairs outside the study area and fledged naturally.

During the study, Runde calculated that the productivity rate per occupied nest site for all territories was 2.47. This is similar to an average of 2.46 from other studies conducted in the western United States. Productivity per successful nest (excluding pairs that failed to produce young) was 3.65. This is slightly above the average of other western studies of 3.49.

In order to calculate the recruitment standard, Runde had to determine the age of first breeding for the population he studied. He knew that one-year-old birds frequently nested in Colorado. These young females achieved an 80 percent nest success and produced the same number of young as older birds. He also observed first-year birds nesting in Wyoming.

If Runde assumed the age at first breeding was two years, the observed productivity for most falcon populations was below the recruitment standard of three birds per nest. This suggests that Prairie Falcon populations are declining throughout the West, which is not the case. It appears that first-year birds do make a significant contribution to the population's stability and that the recruitment standard is really 2–2.5 young per nest. The productivity rate of 2.46 that Runde documented suggests there are surplus birds for harvest.

Runde found that removing young birds from the treatment area did not affect occupancy rates. Two birds were taken from nests for eight years with no measurable impact on the population. Comparisons between the treatment and control areas showed that populations remained relatively stable through the entire study period. Although many local variations exist, a recruitment standard of approximately two young per nest should maintain stable Prairie Falcon populations.

In addition to determining recruitment standards, Runde also studied the turnover rate of adults at specific territories. He found that annual adult mortality was approximately 18 percent. Adults from this population lived approximately four to five years. Fidelity to their nest territories was about 80 percent; in other words, most birds return to the same territory year after year.

Sources

I. SPRING ARRIVAL

Spring Arrival on Nesting Territories: White and Roseneau 1970; Fyfe 1972; Bammann and Doremus 1982; Enderson 1964; Leedy 1972; Denton 1975.

Courtship: Fyfe 1972; Enderson 1964; Wredge and Cade 1977; Cade 1960; Holthuijzen 1992; Birkhead and Lessells 1988; Sodhi 1991; Moller 1987; Balgooyen 1976; Birkhead, Atkin, and Moller 1987.

Seasonal Timing of Nesting: Cade 1982; Williams 1985; Haak 1982.

Nesting: Denton 1975; Enderson, Temple, and Swartz 1973; Newton 1979; Bent 1938; Cade 1982; Edwards 1973; Runde and Anderson 1986; Enderson 1964; Platt 1975; Ogden 1975; Allen, Murphy, and Steenhof 1986; Morrison and Walton 1980; Squires, Anderson, and Oakleaf 1991; Murie and Michener 1984; Morton and Sherman 1978; Ogden and Hornocker 1977; Ogden 1975.

II. THE SUMMER

The Summer: Newton 1979; Sitter 1983.

Productivity: U.S.D.I.–B.L.M. 1979; Cade 1982; Runde 1987.

Young Nestlings: Sitter 1983; Runde 1987; Cade 1982; Moritisch 1983.

Nestling Mortality: Ogden and Hornocker 1977; Denton 1975; Platt 1975; Sitter 1983.

Fledging: Denton 1975; Sitter 1983.

III. FALL AND WINTER DISPERSAL

Fall and Winter Dispersal: Steenhof, Kochert, and Moritsch 1984; Marti and Braun 1975; Enderson 1964; Runde 1987; Newton and Marquiss 1983; Mead 1973, cited in Newton 1979; Mearns and Newton 1984; Greenwood 1980.

Winter Biology: Newton 1979; A.O.U. 1983; Steenhof, Kochert, and Moritsch 1984; Enderson 1964.

Recruitment Standard: Runde 1987; Conway, Runde, Abbite, and Anderson 1993; Webster 1944; Platt 1977; Platt 1981.

CHAPTER 3

Prairie Falcons
and Other Raptors

I
PRAIRIE FALCON CHARACTERISTICS

*P*rairie Falcons have a number of characteristics that distinguish them from other raptors—falcons, hawks, vultures, and owls (Figure 7). When you see a hawk that you wish to identify, the first step is not to immediately start riffling through guide books. It is to observe the bird carefully while making mental notes concerning flight behavior, wing position, and habitat. After careful observation, the next step is to determine the general category.

Eagles (Family Accipitridae)

The two species of eagles, Bald and Golden, are very large, dark-brown raptors with proportionally longer wings. Wing beats are slow and powerful, with the wings held nearly horizontal. They appear steady in flight and do not "totter" like Turkey Vultures. Bald and Golden Eagles are similar in size, with the females being larger than the males in both species (Figure 7).

Vultures (Family Cathartidae)

Vultures are large, dark-colored raptors with heads that lack feathering. They spend many hours gracefully soaring on long wings in search of carrion. Although they have powerful bills for tearing food, their weak feet are not used for grasping prey. In flight, vultures may fly with their wings held in a dihedral or V shape. They are often gregarious, roosting and feeding together, but are solitary nesters (Figure 7).

FIGURE 7
Raptor silhouettes

1. Eagle

2. Vulture

3. Harrier

4. Buteo (soaring hawks)

5. Accipiter (forest hawks)

6. Osprey

7. Falcon

Osprey (Pandionidae)

Ospreys are large raptors usually found near water, where they forage on fish. The characteristic crooked or gull-shaped wing is diagnostic. Ospreys differ anatomically from other raptors in the families Accipitridae, Cathartidae, and Falconidae by their adaptations for catching fish (Figure 7).

Harrier (genus Circus)

The Northern Harrier is the only species of harrier present in North America. Their long, narrow wings are held in a V shape extending above the horizontal. They are medium-sized raptors with long legs and tails. Harriers fly with a low, quartering flight pattern that differs from other raptors. Harriers also have an owl-like facial disk (Figure 7).

Accipiters (genus Accipiter)

The three accipiter species (true hawks) present in North America are all forest hawks that have relatively short, rounded wings and long tails. The wing tips extend only halfway down the tail of perched birds. Accipiter flight is characterized by several rapid wing beats followed by short glides. Although they are very aggressive when defending nesting territories and pursuing prey, accipiters are usually secretive and very difficult to observe (Figure 7).

Buteos (genus Buteo)

Buteo hawks are called "buzzards" in other countries. Unfortunately, in this country, the term *buzzard* is commonly misused to refer to vultures. Buteos are medium- to large-sized raptors that have long, broad wings with relatively short, broad tails. When perched, the wing tips of buteos extend almost the length of the tail. Buteos are conspicuous raptors that are often observed soaring in open habitats or "still hunting" from trees or power poles. Some buteos may have different color morphs in the same areas as normally colored individuals. This diverse coloration can at times frustrate attempts to identify them (Figure 7).

Falcons (genus Falco*)*

Falcons are small to large raptors with relatively long narrow wings, long tails, and broad compact heads. They are rapid fliers with quick wing beats and short glides. The birds prefer open country but often are observed perching in trees or on power poles. When perched, the wing tips extend past half the tail length (Figure 7).

Falcons share a number of similarities with other groups of raptors. They have strong, raptorial feet with a hallux (hind toe) opposite the three forward toes, especially adapted for grasping prey. Their bills are hooked and are very strong. They can easily pull apart the flesh of rabbits, other small mammals, and birds.

After identifying the general type of raptor observed, the next step is to note field characteristics. Important field characteristics of perched birds include color patterns on the belly and back, eye coloration, and banding patterns on the tail. It is also important to note if the leg is feathered and how far down the tail the wing tips extend. When raptors are flying, look for distinctive underwing patterns such as the color of secondaries, banding across the chest or tail, and dark patagial patches (see Figure 7), as well as differing coloration along the wing margins. Also note the relative length of wings and tails, and the size of the head. Only after observing the raptor's general shape, flight behaviors, and distinctive field characteristics are you ready to examine field guides to determine the species.

Characteristics of Prairie Falcons and Other Members of the Genus Falco

Prairie Falcons share a number of characteristics common to other falcons. Their wings are long and narrow with pointed tips, which contrast sharply with the broad, rounded wings of hawks and eagles. Prairie Falcons have low-camber (flat profile) wings with narrow tips that are often swept back along the body, reminiscent of modern jet fighters. The base of the wing also has a pronounced flaring that blends the wing's trailing edge to the body. During rapid flight, their low-camber wings and flarings are superb adaptations that increase efficiency by reducing turbulence and drag. Other birds that either make long migrations or actively feed on the wing, such as swifts, swallows, shorebirds, and hummingbirds, have similar wing profiles.

The Prairie Falcon's chest or pectoral region is also well adapted for rapid flight. Falcons have large keels on their sternums, providing strong anchorage for their powerful flight muscles. Large keels are characteristic of birds that are strong fliers, like pigeons and doves. Flightless birds have only a small keel, or as in the case of the ostrich, none at all. Even within the genus *Falco,* species that are weaker fliers, such as kestrels, have relatively smaller pectoral muscles compared to powerful fliers like Peregrine Falcons.

Falcons have strong, rigid bodies with fused thoracic vertebrae. Their short necks contain only fifteen cervical vertebrae, which gives them a short, compact appearance when viewed from a distance. Falcons also carry an extra pair of bones attached at the base of the tail (pygostyle) that are unique to the family Falconidae. These bones provide a large surface area for attaching the powerful depressor and abductor muscles of the tail. Muscular tails are highly adaptive for birds that twist, turn, and brake sharply when pursuing quarry during high-speed chases. Similar structures occur in some hummingbirds that also depend on maneuverability and braking.

FIGURE 8
Ventral view of flying falcon

1. *Tail or rectrices*   4. *Secondaries*

2. *Undertail coverts*   5. *Primaries*

3. *Axillaries*   6. *Underwing coverts*

The flight feathers of Prairie Falcons have stiff quills that are adapted to cut through the air. Maintaining the condition of these feathers is critical to the falcon's survival and is accomplished by replacing or molting the flight feathers once a year. Falcons have 10 primaries and 11–15 secondaries, which they molt in a pattern that differs from other raptors (see Figure 8). Falcons molt their primaries in both ascendant (toward the wing tip) and descendent (toward the body) order, starting with the fourth primary. The same molting pattern is true for their secondaries, but feather drop starts with the fifth feather.

Prairie Falcons have six pairs of feathers (rectrices) that form a narrow-shaped tail. The tip of the tail in falcons is squarish to rounded, depending on the species. Faster-flying falcons tend to have squarish tails, whereas the tails of slower falcons are more rounded. Falcons initially molt the central pair of tail feathers in an outward progression, except for the outermost feathers (sixth pair), which usually drop before the fifth pair.

The feather tracts on falcons are also arranged differently on their bodies than on other raptors. As the result of these differences, falcons have two brood patches for incubating eggs, whereas eagles and hawks only have one.

Like hawks and eagles, Prairie Falcons have gripping feet equipped with sharp talons that are highly adapted for seizing prey (see Figure 9). However, their feet are less muscular than those of hawks and eagles because they use different methods for killing prey. When hawks or eagles grip prey, they spasmodically clutch their powerful feet, driving their talons deep into their quarry. Prairie Falcons rarely kill prey with their feet. Instead, they bite their quarry in the hind neck, separating the prey's vertebrae with their short, powerful beaks. Even small, robin-sized falcons like kestrels can deliver substantial bites—a fact to which many bird banders can attest. Prairie Falcons have beaks equipped with "tomial teeth," or notches in their upper and lower mandibles which are adaptations for separating the vertebrae of prey.

The eggshells of falcons differ chemically from most other raptors except ospreys, and they lack the usual small cavities (vacuoles). Therefore, when falcon eggs are held to the light, they show a reddish-yellow translucence.

The Prairie Falcon of the western United States is well adapted to its important role in an arid ecosystem. By studying its evolution and behavior, we can learn how this magnificent species survives in the western deserts.

II
EVOLUTION

Falcon Evolution

Because the body parts of Prairie Falcons are so fragile, evolutionary records of the bird and its ancestors are scant. We can, however, look at the evolution of birds in general, including other falcons, in an attempt to reconstruct Prairie Falcon evolution. To do so is an interesting game—like putting a puzzle together.

During the Mesozoic era, more than 130 million years ago, reptiles dominated life on the earth (see Table 5). Scientists believe that sometime during the mid-Jurassic period, birds evolved from reptiles. The first birds were more like flying reptiles: their "flight" consisted of either gliding from tree to tree or jumping to the ground with forelimbs extended. These animals developed enlarged scales—the precursors of feathers.

Scientists believe that during the Jurassic era, Archaeopteryx formed an important link between reptiles and birds. The fossils show that Archaeopteryx was the size of a pigeon, with short legs and a long lizardlike tail. The bird's feathering enabled it to make short, gliding flights. Claws on the wings indicate that Archaeopteryx probably used trees for perches. Its feet also had claws, which suggests it perched in trees.

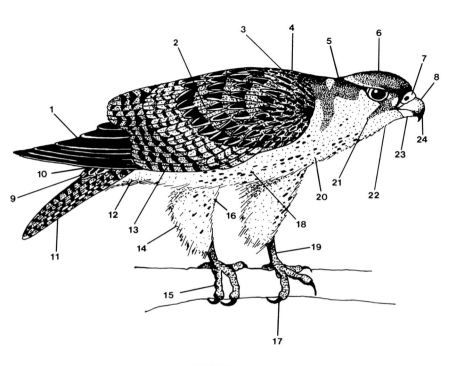

FIGURE 9
Topography of falcon

1. Primaries
2. Upperwing coverts
3. Scapulars
4. Back
5. Nape
6. Crown
7. Cere
8. Upper mandible
9. Upper tail coverts
10. Rump
11. Tail or rectrices
12. Undertail coverts

13. Secondaries
14. Flank feathers
15. Toes and foot
16. Thigh
17. Talon
18. Belly
19. Leg or tarsus
20. Breast
21. Moustacial stripe
22. Throat
23. Lower mandible
24. Notched beak

Around 130 million years ago, a number of birds primarily associated with water began to appear. It is not clear whether this group evolved from Archaeopteryx or from other reptiles. One of the early birds specialized for swimming and diving was the Hesperornis. The teeth in its jaw appear to have been useful for grasping and holding fish. This bird, which resembled modern cormorants, had a long flexible neck and a relatively short tail.

Another early aquatic bird was the Ichthyornis. This animal was gull-like and lived on fish it apparently captured. According to scientists, Ichthyornis, as well as Hesperornis, disappeared as inland waterways receded.

For the late Mesozoic era (the Cretaceous period in the geological timetable), biologists have identified thirty-three species of birds. Included in this group are diving birds, primitive flamingos, loons, grebes, and rail-like birds, as well as early pelicans and gulls.

This early assemblage of birds gave rise to many of the birds that we know today, including the Prairie Falcon. During the Cenozoic era, a large number of birds, such as pelicans, ostriches, albatrosses, storks, ducks, hawks, eagles, pheasants, cranes, terns, cuckoos, woodpeckers, and starlings evolved; presumably, this diversity of new species was in response to a changing climate. As we began to approach the modern era, some birds, such as the ostrich, lost the ability to fly. Large expanses of forests appeared, and land upwellings created extensive grasslands and deserts. Some thirteen million years ago, birds reached their maximum number of species. Since that time, few new forms have evolved, and many have become extinct. Today, there are some 8,900 species of birds, although this number is declining as some species face extinction, especially those on oceanic islands.

Bird evolution can be thought of as a tree whose roots come from Archaeopteryx or other species, and from whose trunk a variety of different species evolved. One of these evolutionary branches included the order Falconiformes. Although modern taxonomists are not in complete agreement, we can look at this

TABLE 5

Geological Time Scale

PERIOD/EPOCH	YEARS SINCE BEGINNING	MAJOR EVENT
Precambrian era		
	4.6 B [a]	Origin of Earth
Paleozoic era		
Cambrian	600 M	Major invertebrate groups present
Ordovician	500 M	Jawless fish
Silurian	425 M	Terrestrial plants
Devonian	400 M	Seed plants
Mississippian	350 M	Amphibians
Pennsylvanian	320 M	Reptiles/Insects
Permian	270 M	Reptiles expand
Mesozoic era		
Triassic	220 M	Amphibians/Dinosaurs
Jurassic	180 M	First birds
Cretaceous	130 M	First primates
Cenozoic era		
Tertiary		
Paleocene	65 M	Mammals and birds
Eocene	55 M	Major bird evolution
Oligocene	36 M	Forest and waterbirds
Miocene	25 M	Major bird groups present
Pliocene	13 M	Height of bird evolution
Quaternary		
Pleistocene	2 M	Falconiformes common
Holocene	11 T	Modern birds

[a] B = Billion
M = Million
T = Thousand

group of birds as one that took advantage of the ability to prey on small mammals and other small birds. Tom Cade, in his excellent book *The Falcons of the World,* discusses the evolution and relationships of different members of the genus *Falco.* Falcons are thought to have evolved in the New World, possibly, as Cade believes, from a South American ancestral raptor with feet that could hold prey but not clutch it. Falcons then radiated worldwide, based on available foraging habitat.

Some falcons, such as the Caracara line, tended towards scavenging; other falcons evolved into efficient aerial predators by becoming smaller and more efficient aerodynamically. Cade postulates that some species of Falconidae, such as species of Caracaras, Forest Falcons (*Micrastur spp.*), and the snake-eating neotropical Laughing Falcon (*Herpetotheres cachinnans*), may still possess some characteristics of ancient forms. According to Cade there are thirty-nine species of falcons in the world.

Biolgists believe that falcons evolved about twenty million years ago, in the Miocene epoch. It appears there were two waves of falcon evolution. First, species like Caracaras, Forest Falcons, and Laughing Falcons spread as they adapted to the tropics. Then, as changing climates created more grasslands, a second wave of falcon evolution occurred, favoring birds better adapted to open areas. Some species of grassland falcons secondarily adapted to arboreal habitats as some forest falcons met extinction. Falcons adapted to open habitats evolved rapidly as grasslands and savannas opened new areas for these predatory birds to hunt; forested areas provided refuge and, in some cases, nesting sites.

The resulting thirty-nine species of falcons we know today are grouped by Cade into eight related groups (subgenera). He groups the large falcons, including the Peregrine, Barbary, and Pallid Falcons, into the subgenus *Rhynchodon.* This group is highly adapted to catching prey in the air. The next subgenus, *Hierofalco,* are desert falcons that exploit dry climatic areas throughout the world. As we discussed, five of the species—

Gyrfalcon, Saker, Lanner, Laggar, and Prairie—occupy similar habitats in different world regions. Two Australian species, the Black and the Gray Falcon, are also placed in this group. These two species prey on reptiles, birds, and mammals.

The subgenus *Nesierax* contains four falcons, including Orange-breasted, Bat, and Aplomado Falcons of the neotropics, and the New Zealand Falcon. Characteristics of species in this group are less unifying than the other groups.

The Merlin, seen throughout the northern parts of the American and Asiatic continents, is in the subgenus *Aesalon*. It is separated taxonomically from the Red-headed Falcon of Africa and India, which is similar in size.

Hobbies are placed in the subgenus *Hypotriorchis* along with the Red-footed and Teita Falcons. These aerial hunters capture flying insects, birds, and bats. Hobbies have the longest and narrowest wings of all falcons.

Under the subgenus *Tinnunculus,* Cade groups ten species that are all part of the kestrel lineage that includes long-winged falcons. In most, plumage color is different in males and females (dimorphic), but the sexes show little size difference. The Common, Moluccan, Australian, American, Madagascar, Mauritius, Seychelles, Lesser, Fox, and Greater Kestrels are all part of this group. Madagascar, Mauritius, and Seychelles Kestrels have very limited distribution, primarily on the islands for which each species was named.

Grey, Dickinson's, and Barred Kestrels of Africa and Madagascar are placed in a group by themselves (subgenus Kestrels), because taxonomists cannot clearly see their relationship to the *Tinnunculus* subgenus. The Brown Falcon of Australia is also set apart from other falcons in the subgenus *Hieaadea* because of its morphology.

Evolution of each species was dependent on its ability to colonize and thrive in an area as the world's climate changed. Desert falcons, including Prairie Falcons, are adapted to the arid inland continents, where a lack of moisture created grass- and brush-land. In all likelihood, the grassland falcons did not have an immediate common ancestor but evolved from forest-type falcons near the open areas they now inhabit.

Taxonomy

Taxonomy is the study of relationships among living organisms. Taxonomists try to find evolutionary characteristics that relate groups of organisms and individual species. To do this, they break down the animal kingdom into groups that share similar characteristics. Thus, the Prairie Falcon is classified as follows: kingdom, Animalia; phylum, Chordata; class, Aves; order, Falconiformes; family, Falconidae; genus, *Falco;* species, *mexicanus.*

Included in the Falconiformes are five families (see Figure 10):

- Cathartidae—7 species of Western Hemisphere vultures;
- Sagittariidae—the Secretary Bird found in Africa;
- Accipitridae—217 species of eagles, hawks, kites, Old World vultures, and harriers found throughout the world;
- Pandionidae—Ospreys found worldwide; and
- Falconidae—Caracaras and falcons.

Vultures in the family Cathartidae typically feed on carrion or dead animals. In the United States, the three vulture species are the Black Vulture, Turkey Vulture, and the endangered California Condor. Secretary birds of Africa (family Sagittariidae), with their long legs and hawklike heads, feed on ground-dwelling reptiles, primarily snakes. The lone occupant of the family Pandionidae—the Osprey—is found along waterways, where it captures fish. The crook in the long wings makes it easy to identify. Ospreys are primarily fish eaters and make large stick nests on poles or treetops near bodies of water.

The family Accipitridae has the largest number of species in the order Falconiformes. Within this family are the three species of accipiters found in North America—Goshawks, Cooper's

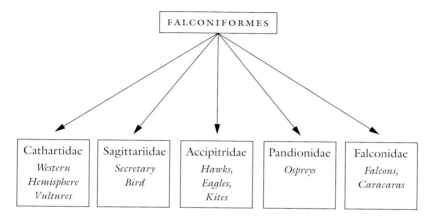

FIGURE 10
Families of falconiformes

Hawks, and Sharp-shinned Hawks. These are long-tailed hunting birds built for maneuvering easily in forested environments. They feed mostly on birds and small mammals. Harriers are also able to maneuver easily. In the United States, the Northern Harrier is found in marshes and grasslands, where it feeds on rodents. Kites are medium-sized, hawklike birds capable of effortless soaring. They generally hover while hunting. Some have very general diets of rodents and insects, whereas the Snail Kite feeds only on one species of snail. Buteos are soaring hawks. North American buteos include Rough-legged, Ferruginous, Red-tailed, Swainson's, and Red-shouldered Hawks, as well as eagles. They often circle for hours before suddenly diving to capture small mammals. Two species of eagles are found in the United States—the Golden and Bald. Golden Eagles feed on rodents and rabbits. Bald Eagles feed primarily on fish and carrion. Immature Bald and Golden Eagles are difficult to distinguish.

The Caracaras share the family Falconidae with falcons. Caracaras are relatively uncommon long-legged birds that can run rapidly on the ground.

III
OTHER DESERT FALCONS

Prairie Falcons evolved in the deserts of the western United States. Surprisingly, they are very similar to other desert falcons around the world. This group of falcons has become adapted to low water and the life cycles of prey populations. All desert falcons utilize similar nesting areas and seek similar types of food. They all must be able to survive in years of scarce food. They all have long wings for maneuverability and strong feet for carrying prey. Desert falcons frequently soar if conditions are right, but they are also very swift fliers. As human populations encroach on desert habitats, desert falcons are all vulnerable to disturbance.

Gyrfalcon (Jur'fal'kon)

The Gyrfalcon is found throughout the world's arctic regions. It breeds in Alaska, northern Canada, around the fringes of Greenland, throughout parts of Scandinavia, and in the northern portion of the former Soviet Union. In very harsh winters, the birds migrate south; however, they usually winter along the edges of boreal forests from western Canada to Labrador, or to just south of the Arctic Ocean; they also winter throughout most of Russia. Gyrfalcons are large, majestic, long-winged hawks. Their coloration ranges from almost pure white to dark black. In fact, taxonomists used to separate some of these birds into separate subspecies that are now all combined. The Gyrfalcon is a very popular bird among falconers. Many Near Eastern falconers will pay large sums of money for the white Gyrfalcon; this falcon used to sell for as much as ten thousand dollars, but prices have declined as more birds became available through captive breeding.

Gyrfalcons breed in a variety of habitats determined primarily by the availability of nest sites and prey. They prefer to nest on cliffs that overlook open tundra; however, some tree-nesting populations have been found in Canada, northern Europe, and Asia. Gyrfalcons are found primarily in three general habitats: near the ocean, along river systems, and on the edge of forests. All provide adequate space for hunting birds and small mammals that inhabit open areas. Winter foods include ptarmigan, grouse, and ducks. Because the arctic climate is so harsh, populations of Gyrfalcons fluctuate widely from year to year. These fluctuations often coincide with cycles in prey populations, causing some wintering Gyrfalcons to move considerable distances in years when prey is sparse. Wintering Gyrfalcons are regularly sighted by bird watchers in the northern United States.

Gyrfalcons are powerful fliers, often searching out prey from a rock perch. Once prey moves, the Gyrfalcon flies from its perch in low, fast pursuit like a plane avoiding radar detection. Hunting Gyrfalcons maneuver behind terrain features in order to conceal their approach. Once close to the prey, they plunge rapidly to grip their quarry. Gyrfalcons also chase down birds until they are exhausted and easily captured.

Most people have never traveled to the Arctic to see Gyrfalcons. But Gyrfalcons are sometimes seen on the western plains during the winter. In parts of its range the Gyrfalcon has been replaced by other falcons, particularly the Peregrine.

Saker (Say'ker)

The Saker is another favorite hunting bird of Arab falconers. It is a smaller, rough-and-tumble version of the Gyrfalcon and can survive in harsh desert regions. Arabian falconers use Sakers to follow large-sized prey for long distances in the desert. These birds lead their handlers to larger prey that they can kill for the dinner table. Sakers nest in parklands and open forests at the edge of the tree line, from eastern Europe throughout the semidesert areas and forests of central Asia. The bird has variable coloration, ranging from pale cream or straw to a uniform chocolate brown. Brown-eyed, light-phase birds are sometimes found and are most prized by falconers.

Sakers often build stick nests in trees. They are very aggressive birds and will drive away other raptors, such as eagles and vultures, from their nests before moving into a new territory. Sakers primarily feed on small mammals, birds, and lizards that they kill in open areas; typically, attacks on prey are initiated from a rock perch, stump, or other high vantage point. Once prey is located, Sakers are very aggressive in their attacks.

In the deserts of north-central Asia, the Saker is the dominant desert falcon. They migrate to southern Asia and parts of Africa for the winter. Biologists find that there are great similarities between the morphology and behavior of the Gyrfalcon and Saker. They presume the two species are very close genetically.

Lanner (Lan'er)

Lanners are falcons of the African deserts. In a disjunct distribution, Lanners inhabit the deserts of North Africa, the Middle Coast, and parts of southern Africa. These birds were once abundant in parts of southern Europe but are now rarely seen.

Lanners are similar to most desert falcons but are most closely related to the Laggar of India. The coloration of this species is variable throughout its range. In southern Africa, the birds are quite handsome, with a line above the eyes and another extending down through the eyes. The brownish breast shaded with black and the blue-gray head create a distinctive impression. Northern birds have a more uniform, lighter-colored pattern.

Lanners eat mainly small mammals, birds, and reptiles. They hunt bats, including the fruit-eating bats that forage in the early evening. They use concealed rock outcrops, trees, or hillside perches from which they swoop down quietly on their prey. They hunt primarily near waterholes, where prey are vulnerable.

Frequently, Lanners remain paired throughout the year, hunting cooperatively. They become more nomadic in the non-breeding season but do not have a true migration to winter areas. Their nests are often at cliff indentations; in some cases they use stick nests built by crows. Lanners, like the Peregrine, will also nest on buildings. When properly trained, Lanners are successfully used for falconry.

Laggar (Lag'gar)

The Laggar is the ecological equivalent to the Lanner on the Indian subcontinent. This bird is distributed south from the Himalayas and Afghanistan through central Burma. Habitats range from dry, open environments to open areas with high moisture. The open country they prefer includes areas cultivated by humans. These birds also live in open forests but avoid densely forested areas.

Laggars are used for falconry, but because they hesitate when attacking prey, their hunting reputation is not as renowned as those of other desert falcons. In some parts of India and Pakistan, Laggars are captured and used as decoys to trap other birds, such as Sakers and Peregrines, that are better suited for falconry. Nests are situated like those of the Lanner—on rocky cliffs, on dirt mounds along water, and sometimes in the nests of other birds. Laggars will nest close to human activities. They appear to remain paired throughout the year and, like the Lanner, make nomadic movements in the non-breeding period. Prey includes small mammals, birds, reptiles, and insects. They also like to hunt pigeons that are attracted to towns and villages. The adult birds have light rufous heads with distinct black stripes extending from the chin up, around the eyes, and back around the head. The bird is blue-gray; the breast is light white with some pinkish and light stripes on the lower parts. A white throat and upper breast is usual in adults, although coloration is variable throughout their range. Immatures have more breast stripes than do adults.

Sources

I. PRAIRIE FALCON CHARACTERISTICS

Raptors: Heintzelman 1979; Clark, Pramstaller, and Pratt, 1980; Clark and Wheeler, 1987.

Characteristics of Prairie Falcons and Other Members of the Genus Falco: Cade 1982; Cramp, Simmons, Gillmor, Hollom, Hudson, Nicholson, Ogilvie, Olney, Roselaar, Voous, Wallace, and Wattel 1982; Richardson 1972.

II. EVOLUTION

Falcon Evolution: Cade 1982; Fox 1977.

III. OTHER DESERT FALCONS

Gyrfalcon: Cade 1982.
Laggar: Cade 1982.

CHAPTER 4

Prairie Falcons and People

I

FALCONRY

We do not know when humans first began training raptors to capture quarry. The practice of falconry may have developed independently in two or more locations, probably in the Far East (China or Mongolia) and in the Middle East, perhaps as early as 2000 B.C. Falconry has ancient roots in Iran and Arabia, but records are scarce. The earliest authenticated record is from the ruins at Khorsabad in the Near East in what was once Assyria. The bas-relief showing a falconer and his hawk dates to around 750 B.C. These nomadic Asians may have discovered that falconry was more efficient in securing food than hunting with bows and arrows. By the second century A.D., falconry was practiced in India; accounts of hunting with trained falcons in China date back as early as 680 B.C. In Japan, falconry was practiced by 720 A.D.

Falconry reached its pinnacle during a period from approximately 500 to 1500 A.D. in the feudal societies of European Christendom and Islam. Falcons were the most valued possessions of the aristocracy, from the kings of Europe to the maharajahs of India to the shoguns of Japan. Strict laws were passed concerning bird ownership. Brutal punishments, which could include the chopping off of hands and eye-gouging, were meted out to those who harmed wild raptors and their nests or stole another's bird.

Falconry was governed by strict social codes that dictated who was allowed to practice falconry and what birds they could fly. The fifteenth-century *Boke of Saint Albans* describes the required social status for owning various birds. Emperors could relish the power and prowess of eagles. Kings commanded Gyrfalcons; princes flew the "falcon gentle" (the female Peregrine); dukes, earls, and barons owned other Peregrines; knights trained the Saker; and the Lanner went to his squire. Mary, Queen of Scots was allowed to fly her Merlin during her captivity. Lower classes of society flew the "ignoble hawks": the female Goshawk for the yeoman; the male Goshawk for the poor man; female Sparrowhawk for the priest; and the muskayte or male Sparrowhawk for the holy water clerk.

Falcons and falconry were a passion that permeated every aspect of medieval life. They were taken into battle and given as peace offerings. During the Crusades, time was taken between battles to go hawking. In fact, Emperor Frederick II of Hohenstaufen (1194–1250) lost an important battle when he took time off to go hawking. Falcons were present in the courts and were carried into churches by the nuns. Many famous leaders, including Genghis Khan, the French kings from Charles VI to Louis XVI, and Russian czars, maintained impressive falconry establishments. Frederick II, who was possibly the greatest falconer ever, introduced the first scientific research on birds in his famous book *De Arte Venandia cum Avibus*. For a thousand years, falcons were woven into the social fabric of daily life to a degree never replicated in our history. The close relationship between birds of prey and humans through falconry was most ably described by Roger Tory Peterson in 1948:

> Man has emerged from the shadows of antiquity with a peregrine on his wrist. Its dispassionate brown eyes, more than those of any other bird, have been witness to the struggle for civilization, from the squalid tents of the steppes of Asia thousands of years ago to the marble halls of European kings in the seventeenth century.

From the seventeenth through nineteenth centuries, the advent of guns and game preserves, along with the general decline of the feudal system, reversed falconry's popularity. Social attitudes toward falcons changed from admiration to contempt. Birds of prey were considered "vermin"; they were shot, poisoned, trapped, and their nests destroyed whenever possible.

In North America, falconry was only practiced to a limited degree until after World War II. Yet today, Tom Cade believes that falconry has never been more popular. He estimates that there are between ten and twenty thousand falconers, most of whom live in North America, Europe, and the Middle East.

Falconry's growing popularity has resulted in the passage of strict regulations designed to protect wild raptor populations. Falconers must pass mandatory tests before they are allowed to take raptors from the wild. Their years of experience determine which species they can fly. In North America, species typically used for falconry include Red-tailed Hawk, Goshawk, Harris Hawk, American Kestrel, Prairie Falcon, and Peregrine Falcon. Organizations such as the North American Falconers' Association, the British Falconers' Club, and the International Association for Falconry and Conservation of Birds of Prey have been instrumental in setting guidelines that regulate falconry. Much to their credit, these organizations have set high standards for their sport. Falconers, by and large, are very knowledgeable about raptor biology and strongly support conservation efforts.

Some people oppose falconry on the basis that it is cruel to keep wild animals in captivity. A trained falcon, unlike a caged parrot, flies free on a regular basis. When prey is sighted, the falcon is released, and it soars high above the falconer. Once free, birds are permitted to leave, and many do. It has been estimated that more than 40 percent of all birds flown in Great Britain are eventually lost to the wild. Falconers voluntarily free another 30 percent of captive birds.

Others oppose falconry by pointing out that taking birds from the wild reduces breeding stocks. This is a valid concern, and in some local situations it may be true. When Peregrine populations declined due to organochlorine pesticides, falconry harvests were curtailed. Most falconers strongly supported these restrictions. Such concerns have lessened, however, as captive breeding increases. Currently in North America, more than half of large falcons used for falconry are bred in captivity,

Immature Prairie Falcon on falconer's glove, hooded. *Photo by Rick Kline*

Recently trapped adult falcon. *Photo by Rick Kline*

easing the demand for wild birds. This trend will increase in the future as advances in captive breeding make these birds readily available and less expensive.

Today's falconers use much of the same equipment that their predecessors created centuries ago. Hoods made of soft leather are placed over the bird's head. They vary from simple, utilitarian designs to elaborate works of art adorned with feathered finery. Hoods prevent the birds from being startled by sudden sights such as an approaching person or vehicle and allow falconers to control high-strung birds—some accipiters, for example—in stressful situations. Short leather thongs called "jesses," which the falconer grasps to control the bird, are attached around the falcon's legs. The jesses are slipped through a figure-eight swivel, which is in turn attached to a leather leash. The leash is tied to a perch that restrains the bird when it is not being flown.

Since birds are completely free when they are flown, it is sometimes difficult for falconers to keep track of their birds. Traditionally, bells were tied to the birds' legs. The ringing of the two-tone bells can be heard from a great distance and assists falconers in their search for lost birds. The music created by a falcon's bells during flight is an alluring sound that is long remembered. However, many falconers have replaced their bells with miniature radio transmitters. Radio transmitters are better than bells for locating lost birds, because the signal can be received many miles away.

The first phase of training a bird usually entails teaching it to perch on the glove. During this taming or "manning" process, the bird must be carried for long periods and introduced to the sights and sounds of captivity. The bird also learns to feed comfortably from the fist and begins to build trust with the falconer. After the falcon becomes more relaxed in the falconer's presence, it is encouraged to fly increasing distances to the fist for food. A light cord, called a creance, is attached to the jesses so the bird can fly longer distances while remaining secured. When the bird flies the length of the creance with confidence, the cord is removed and the bird flies free. Next, the falcon is introduced to the lure, which serves as an artificial quarry. The falconer swings the lure in circles on a short line while the stooping falcon tries to strike it. Once the falcon successfully hits the lure, it is allowed to feed. Lure flying is tough work for a falcon. It may make fifty passes before "capturing" the lure.

Lure flying is valuable experience for some species of falcons. However, it may be detrimental to Prairie Falcons because it encourages them to fly at low altitudes when hunting game, which they tend to do naturally. Falconers want their birds to hunt high above the ground to increase their success in capturing quarry and to produce more thrilling flights.

The culmination of the training process is to hunt quarry with the trained falcon. Falcons are usually hunted in open country where visibility is good and there is lots of room for flights. The falconer, normally with the aid of a good dog, searches for potential quarry. Once the dog freezes in a "point" position, the falconer casts off the falcon from the fist. The bird circles high overhead and "waits on" the falconer to flush the quarry. Experienced falcons watch the dog keenly waiting for the quarry to flush. Once the quarry flushes, the falcon folds its wings and plummets toward the prey. Falcons sometimes strike and daze a large prey before killing it on the ground; small prey are forced to the ground and speedily dispatched with a quick bite to the neck.

Falcons are often unable to capture the intended quarry. Part of the challenge of falconry is that the quarry often escapes. The falconer enjoys the privilege of watching the interactions of predator and prey. Sometimes the falcon captures the prey; other times the falcon is left calling in frustration as the prey escapes.

Falconry requires a significant commitment from the falconer in terms of time and money. It becomes a lifestyle rather than just a sport. Falconers must be willing to spend hundreds of hours training and maintaining their birds. Falcons, unlike fly rods or shotguns, cannot be put away on the shelf until the falconer chooses to go afield. Captive raptors require daily attention. In terms of providing meat for the table, falconry is relatively inefficient. Hunters concerned about the amount of wild game on their tables would be wiser to pursue it with a shotgun rather than a falcon. The excitement of falconry lies in watching the interactions between falcon and prey, and the close contact humans achieve with raptors. The falconer becomes merely an observer, a bird-watcher at close range. The success of the flight depends on the skill of the falcon and the skill of the prey. The falconer's reward is simply watching the contest.

Training Prairie Falcons

I (J. R. S.) must admit I listened in disbelief as falconer friends described Prairie Falcons as worthy hunting companions. My

personal experience with falconry had been restricted to training hawks, not falcons, so I had many biased opinions concerning the training of Prairie Falcons. Much of the literature suggests that Prairie Falcons are bad-tempered birds known for
their moodiness. Also popular is the notion that they do not
"wait on" the falconer (circle above waiting for quarry to be
flushed) high enough to produce spectacular flights.

My first experience watching a trained Prairie Falcon perform
in the field reconfirmed all my preconceived notions. The bird
was a female eyas (taken as a young nestling and imprinted to
humans) that screamed incessantly. When she fed on the glove,
she hissed, bit, beat her wings frantically, and turned her back
to the falconer; her manners on the fist were atrocious. The falconer told me that eyas Prairie Falcons usually behaved in this
manner. Finally, we located a pond with several mallards near
the shore, and the falcon was released. She flew only 15 meters
off the ground before beginning to stoop at the ducks repeatedly. Eventually, one duck flushed from the pond was struck
and killed by the falcon.

Luckily, the poor behavior and lackluster flight I witnessed
were reflections of the falconer's lack of experience in training
Prairie Falcons, rather than inherent characteristics of the species. Prairie Falcons are one of the premier raptors available for
falconry in North America. They possess an excellent combina-
tion of speed, maneuverability, and indomitable courage and
can produce spectacular flights when hunting quarry. Because
they evolved in the harsh western environment, Prairie Falcons
have the stamina to out-fly the strongest quarry. They have the
spirit to crash through dense cover when attacking prey, something Peregrines seldom attempt. In addition, the Prairie Falcon is really the only large wild falcon (i.e., not hybrid or captive bred) that is sufficiently abundant to be readily available to
the average falconer in North America.

Prairie Falcons' inherent aggression is obvious when they
strike prey. They strike with such force that the quarry is often
stunned or killed by the first blow. Their hard-hitting hunting

behavior is good for game hawking but can result in an injury to the falcon. Some Prairie Falcons will strike geese, and most will strike ducks and pheasants. Falconers that slip their birds on very large quarry risk injury or death to their falcons. Successful falconry with Prairie Falcons requires that the falconer appreciate the unique characteristics of this species. Training methods for Peregrine Falcons may not work with this desert falcon.

Bruce Haak, in his book *The Hunting Falcon*, describes what is required to raise an eyas Prairie Falcon. Proper training will provide the falconer with years of exciting game hawking. Falcons taken as young chicks will imprint to the falconer and become very tame compared to birds captured as sub-adults. Haak explains it is critically important that the growing eyas always have food available. The young nestling should feed freely from the lure and glove. During this time, the falconer needs to establish close ties with the young Prairie Falcon. The bird needs to be constantly exposed to people, dogs, cars, and all other features of modern life.

Wild Prairie Falcons scream at parent falcons both as a means of recognition and when begging for food. However, excessive screaming by captive falcons is unmanageable. The captive Prairie Falcon eyas should never scream from hunger, since food should be provided *ad libitum*. In addition, high social interaction between the eyas and the falconer also reduces screaming. Haak believes that well-adjusted eyas do not know fear, insecurity, or loneliness, because they grow up in constant contact with people. This interaction includes holding the young bird to provide physical contact. A maladjusted young Prairie Falcon that grows up bored and hungry is likely to become a screamer. Falcons taken as young eyas should not be returned to the wild, because they are imprinted to humans.

Before the young falcon can fly, it should be allowed to run around the yard under close supervision. It will soon begin making short flights within the familiar territory where it was raised. This is an easy time for the young falcon. It may play with its lure or a ball as it further adjusts to its surroundings. Everything in the young falcon's world becomes "prey" as it learns to attack blowing leaves or a paper cup. This process of "tame-hacking" is an important part of the falcon's development. It allows the youngster to adjust to its new environment on its own terms. In the next week or two, the young falcon will become a stronger flyer and will begin chasing small birds as a means of honing its hunting skills. As the bird further matures, the falconer should encourage it to fly directly overhead as it begins to learn how to "wait on." By twelve weeks of age, the young Prairie Falcon will be ready to fly quite high and kill bagged pigeons and other game as it gains experience. Some falconers do not desire the tameness of an eyas. They prefer trapping a sub-adult falcon (a "passage" bird) that already is a strong flyer and an accomplished hunter. Eyas Prairie Falcons may require four months of intense training before they are hunting game, whereas a passage bird may be hunting game in a matter of weeks.

Passage Prairie Falcons are tamed or "manned" by patiently coaxing the bird to feed from the fist. According to Haak, one of the fastest ways to "man" a passage falcon is by "waking," a technique developed centuries ago. The falcon is carried day and night for two to three days. The bird is fed, stroked, and introduced to our noisy world while becoming more complacent as it grows more exhausted. Compared to a fresh bird, a tired falcon will respond in a milder manner to strange sights. Later, it will more likely take the situation in stride.

Dr. Ken Tuttle has been a falconer for twenty-five years and was the first president of the Utah Falconer's Association. He has flown Prairie Falcons for more than fifteen years and has written numerous articles about their handling and training. He believes that no raptor attacks quarry with more enthusiasm than passage Prairie Falcons. Passage falcons are controlled primarily through regulation of appetite and weight. Dr. Tuttle believes that weight management is critically important when training and flying passage Prairie Falcons (personal communication, 1993).

Prairie Falcons are usually trapped in fat condition. If food is decreased, the newly trapped falcon may fly short distances to the falconer in a matter of two to six days after capture. "Flying weight" is by definition the body weight at which the falcon is a strong flier and is aggressive toward game. The correct flying weight for a given bird is based on the falcon's tameness, amount of exercise, daily temperatures, food consumption, and food quality. If the falcon's weight declines much below its flying weight, it will starve. Most trapped passage female Prairie Falcons weigh 725–855 grams; flying weights usually range from 700 to 765 grams.

Wild Prairie Falcons often hunt game using a low, contour hugging flight, but falconers desire birds that will fly high ("wait-on" overhead) as they wait for game to be flushed. The falconer's task is to encourage this hunting style in his or her tame falcon. Traditionally, falconers have taught their birds to repeatedly stoop at a swung lure as a means of training and conditioning. Peregrine Falcons may benefit from lure flying, but not Prairie Falcons. Bruce Haak has found that Prairie Falcons, with their fierce tempers, do not adjust to having their lure taken from them after a hard flight. He believes the practice of lure flying is the main reason the misconception prevails that Prairie Falcons will not "wait on." In place of lure flying, Dr. Tuttle uses a "vertical" exercise in which the falcon is taught to fly from a very low perch on the ground up to the fist. This method has been used by Arab falconers for centuries and may be better than lure-flying. A falcon that makes more than one hundred vertical flights per session will be in excellent shape for chasing wild game.

Whether training an eyas or passage Prairie Falcon, the ultimate goal is a well-mannered bird that "waits-on" high overhead as it watches the falconer flush game. Once quarry is spotted, the newly trained falcon should have the spirit and courage to attack prey with the ferocity characteristic of their species. Although Prairie Falcons may be short-tempered compared with some large falcons, when properly handled they truly are one of North America's premier game hawks. Experienced falconers with a sensitivity to the Prairie Falcon's unique behavioral characteristics witness stellar flights between their falcons and such capable quarry as pheasants, waterfowl, and several species of upland birds. If managed properly, wild populations of Prairie Falcons can provide falconers a source of excellent game hawks while maintaining the viability of wild falcon populations.

11
CAPTIVE BREEDING

Captive breeding has been a fascinating and valuable wildlife management technique for reestablishing the Peregrine Falcon population. Prairie Falcons have been used as surrogates in the breeding of Peregrines and have played an important role in the development of captive-breeding techniques. Although a German falconer, Waller, had succeeded in breeding a pair of Peregrine Falcons in 1942 and 1943, the first consistent and encouraging results in the captive breeding of raptors were achieved with American and European Kestrels.

Recent advances show that practical, large-scale captive breeding is feasible for most species, including Peregrines. At least fifteen species of *Falco* and three interspecific crosses have produced fertile eggs and successfully reared young in captivity. American Kestrels are especially easy to propagate, as are European Kestrels, and their captive-bred offspring also have been successful in producing young. In addition, larger species, such as Lanners, Peregrines, and Prairie Falcons, have produced captive-bred young that have successfully reproduced. The Gyrfalcon was the most recent of the large species to reproduce in captivity, and it now seems likely that all species of falcons can be bred under the right circumstances.

The Peregrine Fund's research program (a non-profit organization dedicated to reestablishing the Peregrine Falcon) was started through the efforts of Tom Cade at Cornell University in 1970. The goal of this program was to develop techniques necessary for breeding falcons in captivity and to build up a captive population of falcons that would be able to produce a supply of birds sufficient to reestablish Peregrines in the eastern United States. This program has been very successful. Peregrine Falcons are now reestablished throughout much of their original range.

Captive breeding is interesting to observe. Scientists have adopted breeding techniques used in the poultry industry, such as artificial insemination, and applied them to raptors. A male bird is taken into the laboratory and has a cloth placed over its head. A technician gently strokes the male, who is held over a pan, causing it to ejaculate. Semen is then placed into a test tube, where it can be stored up for up to twenty-four hours. When the female falcon is ready for breeding, the male semen is placed into a capillary tube and is carefully inserted into the female's cloaca; the semen is then forced out. This procedure obviously requires a great deal of experience. Tom Cade has studied the best methods to artificially inseminate falcons and has found that the female should have laid an egg no more than twelve hours before the attempt. The biologist generally inseminates after each egg to fertilize the second egg to follow.

After the eggs are laid, Cade and his associates allow the parent bird to incubate them at least seven days. This period of natural incubation helps the eggs survive. The female turns the eggs frequently, which keeps the embryo from attaching to the eggshell and prevents desiccation. After seven days under the parent's care, eggs are placed in an incubator. About forty-eight hours before the chick first pips the shell, the air cell within the egg begins to expand and extend halfway down one side of the egg. Chicks that have not lost sufficient moisture prior to this time may not hatch. When an egg has pipped, it is placed in a hatcher with a slightly lower temperature and a higher relative humidity to prevent desiccation.

Once they have hatched, the Peregrine Falcon hatchlings are raised in captivity for a short period of time and then moved to hack-sites (release sites prepared with release cages) throughout the country. The young are fed in the hack-site until they can be released. Attendants remain at these sites and continue to provide food for the young falcons as long as they return to the sites.

Captive-bred Prairie Falcons have also been successfully reintroduced into the wild. Most releases did not follow the elaborate hacking techniques used on Peregrine Falcons. In 1976, the California Department of Fish and Game placed two captive-bred female Prairie Falcons in a eyrie near Newell, California. The birds were approximately 13–14 days old. The eyrie already contained a young nestling, approximately the same age. Both adult falcons were attending the young bird, and they accepted and fed the additional two birds. All three young birds fledged and were seen foraging for themselves.

Biologists continue to make advances in captive breeding techniques. In the mid-1980s, new procedures were developed for freezing and thawing semen from Peregrine Falcons. In order to test the fertility of semen which had been treated and frozen in liquid nitrogen for at least one year, four female Prairie Falcons with histories of laying eggs in captivity were acquired from falconers and captive breeders. The level of fertility biologists obtained using the stored semen was low, but encouraging. Others have obtained fertility levels of up to 30 percent with frozen kestrel semen using dimethylacetamide as the cryoprotectant rather than the usual glycerol. George Gee (personal communication, 1994) suggested that 50 percent fertility can be obtained with frozen kestrel semen when dimethyl sulfoxide is used as the cryoprotectant. Biologists have been unable to maintain post-thaw viability of Peregrine sperm with either of these cryoprotectants. While these procedures demonstrate that the use of frozen semen is a realistic option in the captive breeding of large falcons, we will need more practical methods for processing Peregrine semen and higher fertility rates before frozen semen will be useful in most captive-breeding situations.

One method of improving semen viability involves a process of imprinting male birds on people. Boyd and his associates report that a male Prairie Falcon was pair-bonded with a man, allowing semen to be collected without artificially shocking the male. This semen was used to inseminate five female Prairie Falcons, all of which produced healthy offspring. Prairie Falcons, therefore, are serving an important role in the development of artificial insemination techniques.

III
PESTICIDES

Pesticides are used to control 2,000 different pests, yet they affect 200,000 non-target species, including raptors. In the last fifty years, several raptor populations have declined throughout the world. Peregrine Falcons, in particular, declined after World War II because of DDT contamination. By the early 1970s, they were completely gone from the eastern United States and were listed as endangered. Today, they have been reintroduced in parts of their range, and their populations are recovering. Other raptor populations have precipitously declined due to loss of habitat from development, poaching, and human disturbance. Although once an endangered species, Bald Eagles have been downlisted as "threatened" through parts of their range in North America.

Types of Pesticides

The term *pesticide* includes such substances as insecticides, herbicides, fungicides, fumigants, algaecides, avicides, and rodenticides, all developed and used to control pest populations. Some of these chemicals are more harmful to birds than others.

Insecticides are a major cause of lasting problems with raptor populations. Although insecticides have had positive effects for humans, like controlling malaria-carrying mosquitoes and destroying the tsetse fly, the side effects to our ecosystem have been severe. In some parts of the world, populations of Peregrine Falcons have been lost. Thus far, Prairie Falcon populations have not been as severely affected. Insecticides are divided into four major classes: inorganics, oils, botanicals, and synthetics.

INORGANICS. Inorganics have been used for some time, although today they have been largely replaced by more efficient organic compounds. Most inorganics, like lead arsenic used on shrubs and trees to control chewing insects, are insect stomach poisons. Sulfur derivatives, Paris green, and calcium arsenate are some others. This whole group is generally restricted in use because of its toxicity to humans and persistence in the environment.

OILS. Oils are petroleum products that are used to coat water, soil, and sometimes plants, to prevent insect emergence.

BOTANICALS. Some plant extracts are used as insecticides. These botanicals are complex chemicals that break down into harmless compounds soon after application. Most are effective in destroying specific insects, usually soft-bodied ones such as aphids and caterpillars. They are relatively safe for people to handle. Pyrethrin, rotenone, nicotine, and dimethrin are a few common ones.

SYNTHETICS. By far the most-used insecticides today belong to the organic or synthetic group. Use of these synthetics has sparked most of the debate over the effect of insecticides on the environment. Three general chemical groups of organics are: organochlorines (chlorinated hydrocarbons), organophosphates, and carbamates.

Organochlorines, including DDT, dieldrin, and aldrin, have been used since 1945. Although effective in destroying insect pests, they kill other animals as well. They are fat soluble, persistent, mobile, and very stable. Most of the research has been done on DDT, but all organochlorines have similar patterns of activity, with the central nervous system as the main body target. The fatty layer surrounding many nerves appears to absorb organochlorines. Once in the fat, they cause hyperactivity and convulsions by initiating a series of nerve impulses. Scientists believe paralysis and death occur from neural toxicity or the exhaustion of metabolic processes.

Another type of organochlorine with similar structure and chemical properties is polychlorinated biphenyls, or PCBs. PCBs are used in manufacturing rubber, plastics, inks, and carbonless reproducing paper. Although they are not pesticides, PCBs enter the water and atmosphere and pose serious health problems.

Organophosphates are mainly contact insecticides, although some are absorbed through the respiratory system. A variation of Tabun, a nerve gas developed but not used by the Germans during World War II, these organophosphates interfere to various degrees with the transmission of nerve impulses across nerve synapses. A nerve carrying an impulse releases the chemical acetylcholine to stimulate an impulse in the neighboring nerve. The enzyme cholinesterase usually breaks down the acetylcholine, but it is inactivated by organophosphates. This results in continuous stimulation of the nerve until the organism goes into spasms and eventually dies. In higher animals, symptoms such as nausea, salivation, muscle spasm, coma, and convulsions occur. More than forty commercially successful organophosphates, including Azodrin, Parathion, and Malathion, are in this group.

Carbamates are relatively new and represent a unique, greatly diversified class of insecticides known to act synergistically with several other insecticides. They are absorbed on contact or through the stomach wall and apparently deactivate the enzyme cholinesterase, as do organophosphates. These pesticides are rapidly broken down to less toxic chemicals and eliminated from the insect's body, so they do not accumulate in fat. Carbamates such as Furadan, Lunnate, and Sevin are used today to protect a number of agricultural crops.

Throughout much of their range, Peregrines were extirpated as breeders by 1965, eighteen years after the introduction of DDT. In locations where DDT was introduced at a later date, such as in Alaska, biologists were able to correlate Peregrine declines with the increased pesticide use. Wherever a population experienced a 16–18 percent eggshell thinning due to several years' pesticide use, productivity failed and the population declined. Organochlorides also caused the eggs to fail due to poor air exchange and toxic conditions.

Approximately 7.7 million kilograms (1.7 billion pounds) of synthetic organic pesticides are used in the United States each year. Placing this amount uniformly over the United States equals about 52 kilograms (115 pounds) of active pesticides per 4 square kilometers (0.4 square miles). Pesticides are applied as aerosols, liquids, or solids. In all cases, they move into air, soil, water, and living organisms. The atmosphere is considered a major route for the widespread distribution of persistent pesticides. For example, DDT levels in samples from the air around Bermuda in 1974 were one hundred times greater than the levels from samples taken nine years earlier.

Most organochlorines are long-lived and persistent. Fifty percent of the DDT originally applied to fields remain in the

soil after three years. It generally takes ten years for 95 percent
of the DDT to decompose, and traces may be found as late as
thirty years following application. Plants absorb these compounds during this entire period. Animals that eat grasses (herbivores) ingest the chemicals, which are retained in their body
tissue. Predators, like Prairie Falcons, eat the herbivores and accumulate even greater concentrations of chemicals. The accu-
mulation of pesticides as they pass through the food chain is
called biological magnification. Pesticides are usually applied
several times a year, so buildup in the soil and biota causes
significant environmental problems.

Organochlorines are most highly concentrated in fish-eating
birds, followed by (in decreasing order) raptors, omnivorous
birds, and herbivorous birds. Studies on eggs in museums show
that eggshell thickness of bird eggs decreased between 1945
and 1947—the period when DDT was first introduced into
the ecosystem on a worldwide basis. DDT disrupts the body's
mechanism for transporting calcium, thus reducing the thickness of eggshells. Some bird populations, such as the Bald
Eagle, Peregrine Falcon, Osprey, and Brown Pelican, decreased
or disappeared from parts of their range because thinned
eggshells cracked during incubation.

In comparison, organophosphates are unstable, and most
tend to degrade to harmless chemicals after several months. In
general, these compounds are not accumulated or stored in living tissue; however, they are toxic to people in high concentrations and can be a special hazard to the worker applying them.
Greenhouse workers are killed in situations where ventilation
is poor.

Studies show that a variety of pesticides and other toxicants
also accumulate in animals' tissues and interfere with their reproduction. Wood-stork eggs from Florida contain DDE (a
DDT derivative), mercury, and PCBs, and their hatching success was reduced as amounts of DDE increased. Loggerhead
sea turtles also have high DDE concentrations.

Prairie Falcons and Pesticides

Although Prairie Falcons and Peregrine Falcons nest in similar areas of the western United States, Prairie Falcons have not suffered the same declines as Peregrines. In the northwestern United States, fewer than 20 percent of all Peregrine eyries that were active in the 1940s were still occupied in 1965. However, Morley Nelson found that Prairie Falcons continued to be common in suitable habitats in the same region. During the 1960s and 1970s, some Prairie Falcon populations in southern Canada and the western United States may have suffered from the effects of pesticides. Richard Fyfe and his associates collected eggs from areas in Canada where declines had occurred and found measurable residues of organic chloride insecticide. Eggs contained a variety of pesticides and pesticide metabolites, including DDE, DDD, DDT, and others. Their data showed Prairie Falcons accumulated high levels of insecticides, including DDT and dieldrin, after eating highly contaminated food items. This resulted in the body fat of Prairie Falcons having relatively high levels of pesticides, which in turn contaminated their eggs.

Fyfe found that Prairie Falcon eggs contained highly variable levels of pesticide residues, indicating that some birds were selecting prey heavily contaminated with organic chloride pesticides (DDT), while others were not. Because of such tremendous individual variations in pesticide exposure, not all Prairie Falcon populations were affected. Since Prairie Falcons feed on a variety of prey, their exposure to pesticides in a given area can vary according to food type.

Although some Prairie Falcon populations have been subjected to pesticide poisoning, only a few populations have experienced declines. In an attempt to see how pesticides can potentially affect Prairie Falcons, Jim Enderson and Dan Berger fed dieldrin to forty-three of seventy-eight nesting wild female birds by offering them contaminated starlings. Evaluation of

Prairie Falcon hunting habitat. *Photo by LuRay Parker, Wyoming Game and Fish Department*

the eggshell thickness showed that Prairie Falcons accumulated high levels of dieldrin in their body fat after ingesting only a few of the highly contaminated starlings. Dieldrin levels in the eggs of these birds were many times greater than in untreated falcons, and eggshell-thickness reduction occurred after only one season of pesticide ingestion. Although Prairie Falcons can suffer the effects of chlorinated hydrocarbons, relatively few populations have suffered severe declines during periods of heavy pesticide use. This indicates their prey are not exposed to the pesticide levels that affect other raptor populations. Apparently, pesticides are not commonly used in the summer or winter ranges used by Prairie Falcons and their prey.

IV
HABITAT MITIGATION

In parts of the West, people are causing major changes in Prairie Falcon habitat that may threaten populations. The impact of development can alter foraging areas and the prey base on which Prairie Falcons depend. Just the presence of humans can make a difference between successful nesting and survival of young birds or complete failure. There are, however, many ways that people can both enjoy the Prairie Falcon and allow populations to flourish. In this section we look at how humans and falcons interact and discuss how the two might better coexist.

Human Impacts

We believe that road construction may negatively impact Prairie Falcon populations. For example, in Oregon biologists found that 65 percent of eyries were located an average of 1,700 meters from a road. Usually, the roads were graveled or unmaintained access roads that received only light local traffic, but sometimes nests were near paved roads with substantial traffic volumes. One nest was within 50 meters of a primary state highway. Most Prairie Falcons are sensitive to nesting near human habitations. Only 15 percent of eyries were located within 1,760 meters of human habitations.

In areas where Prairie Falcons have frequently nested, mining and oil and gas development may have reduced populations. Again, it appears that road construction, rather than the people responsible for the development, caused the reductions. Often, it is the tourists and hunters who begin to use the area who create disturbances. Also, some people shoot Prairie Falcons. Indiscriminate shooting of Prairie Falcons has greatly impacted some populations. One way of minimizing the harm to Prairie Falcons is to close temporary roads during the breeding season so that the Prairie Falcon population may be left undisturbed at this sensitive time.

Habitat changes in Prairie Falcon foraging areas may be less disruptive to birds than disturbances at nest sites. We examined the movements and habitat-use patterns of a small population of Prairie Falcons that nested near Gillette, Wyoming. These falcons foraged in areas that had approximately 1.5 oil wells per square kilometer. We found that Prairie Falcons did not overtly avoid oil wells when foraging. For example, they did not overfly the entire oil field but appeared to forage in the undisturbed areas between wells.

Although we never observed falcons hunting or perching on the actual drill pad, they did frequently perch on the power poles leading to the wells. Possibly, oil development would have adversely affected their foraging behavior if wells were at a much greater density. The nest sites used by this population were isolated from human disturbance. Oil wells and associated haul roads were not situated on the actual buttes used for nesting but were restricted to the falcons' foraging areas. Landowners also restricted the general public's access to the nesting area. The protection of nesting areas may explain why these birds appeared to be unaffected by oil development. The results from our study suggest that Prairie Falcons can cope with limited energy development on their foraging areas if their eyries are secure from human disturbances.

Construction and mining often involve the use of explosives. In New Mexico, Prairie Falcons subjected to continued blasting did not return in years following the blasts. In the mid-1980s, biologists in Idaho's Birds of Prey National Conservation Area studied how Prairie Falcons reacted to explosions. Birds were observed both before and after explosions to record their reaction. Perched falcons usually made short flights into the canyon in response to blasts. They often perched briefly in a new location in apparent effort to see what was going on. Some falcons remained perched after the blast; others' response was to attack neighboring ravens. Incubating falcons often continued to incubate. Sometimes they sat up and then resumed incubation within a minute or two; a few falcons were flushed briefly from their eyries before returning to incubate. Prairie Falcons changed their behavior following blasting 54 percent of the time. Both male and female falcons responded in a similar manner to blasts. In most cases, the bird simply flew or was flushed away from the area in a kind of a startlement behavior.

In this study, investigators set up experimental blasts in an area away from construction to separate the effects of the two. The results did show differences between experimental and construction blasting. Flushing rates in the experimental location were four to six times higher than those in construction areas. Readjustment times, that is, the time the birds required to adjust to the blast and return to the activities they had been engaged in before the blasting, were similar in both areas. Generally, this period was relatively short, often under three minutes.

All four nesting territories in the experimental study location that were exposed to blasting in 1985 were occupied in 1986, and three pairs successfully fledged young. In 1987 only one of the four nesting territories was occupied and produced five young. The other three nesting territories were vacant. However, the investigators point out that occupancy rates in other areas were also down. Of course, there is always the possibility that some or all of these birds did not survive the winter. The investigators on the Birds of Prey study concluded that construction activities, including blasting, did not have a detectable adverse effect on nesting Prairie Falcons. However, Richard Fyfe and Richard Olendorf, as well as Al Harmata and associates, reported that nesting Prairie Falcons were disturbed by low-intensity human activity over a period of time.

When falcons are disturbed and kept from their eyries, eggs or nestlings may overheat or chill. This can occur if people disturb the birds to such an extent that they will not return to the area within a few minutes; this concern is especially great during midday, when the sun beats down on the eggs. It would also be a concern in the evening, when it is cool.

Prairie Falcon hunting habitat. *Photo by LuRay Parker, Wyoming Game and Fish Department*

The timing of human disturbances is critical to their effect on nesting Prairie Falcons. Some biologists, like Richard Fyfe and Richard Olendorf, suggest that human disturbances just prior to egg laying may cause Prairie Falcons to desert their nests. Field studies show that adult Prairie Falcons are less likely to abandon their nests in the more advanced stages of their nesting cycle when young are present. Again, it may be important to look at the type of disturbance. Prolonged human disturbance, with people in the area, may be more upsetting than occasional blasting.

Powerlines are also dangerous to birds of prey. Large raptors that land on power poles can be electrocuted or caught in the line. This is particularly true of birds such as Golden Eagles. To a lesser extent, Prairie Falcons have been electrocuted by power lines. Power companies have tried to mitigate this problem. They have modified power poles so that they extend above the power lines sufficiently and birds can take off without touching the lines. In areas of particularly heavy bird movement, markers that increase the visibility of the line have effectively reduced bird strikes. This has not been tested extensively with raptors but has been widely tested with cranes and waterfowl. A study of the Platte River in Nebraska found that when yellow marker balls 30 centimeters in diameter were placed between poles, collisions by cranes were reduced significantly. In areas where there might be heavy use or movement of raptors, such techniques might effectively reduce the mortality of birds that strike lines.

Livestock grazing affects Prairie Falcons in terms of prey abundance. Grasses and shrubs are trampled, disturbing the habitat of falcon prey. On the other hand, moderate grazing can benefit prey by opening small corridors between grasses or shrubs so small birds and mammals can move about. Prairie Falcons can use these openings to capture prey. Management of livestock grazing in any of these arid environments can be effective in maintaining the prey population and allowing Prairie Falcons to find small birds and mammals. In some regions, wildlife such as antelope and wild horses may also affect the condition of the range if they are allowed to increase to large numbers.

The prey base is important to the survival of Prairie Falcon. As we saw in the last section, contaminants can affect the food and the biology of the population. Where large-scale rodent poisoning programs have been instituted, the prey base has declined and the Prairie Falcon population lowered. Prairie Falcon predation helps control prey so that poisoning programs are unnecessary.

Mitigation Measures

When nesting habitat has been lost due to energy development, urban expansion, or recreation, new nest sites can be created to partially mitigate habitat loss. In some cases, coal companies leave behind high walls and other cliffs that are used by Prairie Falcons for nesting. On several occasions, Prairie Falcons have quickly colonized these newly formed high-wall areas. If a mine reclamation program plans to create high-wall eyries, designers should consider several factors. Studies have suggested that nest potholes should be located on a south-facing slope about two-thirds up the cliff to best attract the falcons. The floor area of the pothole should be about 7,000 square centimeters with a gentle slope of 5–10° to the front. Overhead cover should be present, and the base slope should be about 54°. Field studies suggest that cliffs or high walls that are retained for raptors should be at least 14 meters tall and should be resitant to water erosion.

Newly created eyries should be clustered together to mimic a nest territory with several alternative nesting sites. Spacing between new territories depends on the presence of visual barriers separating them. When such barriers are present, successful nests may be as close as 150 meters. Doug Runde showed that in a three-year period, over half the eyries in his study area were occupied only once, and 23 percent were occupied every two years. He feels that two or three nest sites should be provided on each cliff. The ability to use alternate eyries within nesting territories may reduce direct competition for nest sites with owls and decrease the frequency of parasitic insects.

Fyfe and Armbruster were able to improve existing cliffs for nesting Prairie Falcons by digging new holes or creating ledges in those cliff faces that had few suitable sites. They selected cliffs based on criteria that included location in relation to suitable prey habitat, freedom from excessive human activity, a relatively permanent or solid substrate of clay or sandstone, and freedom from excessive erosion.

In cliffs that met these criteria, they created falcon nestholes or ledges with minimum dimensions of 30 centimeters deep × 60 centimeters long × 30 centimeters high. Several methods were employed to create nest sites, including the use of dynamite and digging by hand with a small shovel. These generally proved to be inefficient: dynamite dug too large a hole and digging by hand was extremely difficult and time-consuming. Although ineffective, digging by hand with a small shovel proved to be the best method to excavate the cavity.

There has been considerable initial success with creating artificial eyries. In 1970, of five potholes dug into a cliff in Montana, four were occupied by paired Prairie Falcons and a fifth by a lone male Prairie Falcon. Thus, the creation of nest sites in cliffs where nest sites may be limited, or in areas where mine reclamation is occurring, can effectively enhance Prairie Falcon populations. Obviously, prey must also be available to support the populations where new nest sites are created.

In 1978, the U.S. Forest Service constructed a nesting ledge from galvanized angle iron at a cliff site where Peregrine Falcons had nested in California. The ledge had broken off, so it was not large enough to support a new nest. In 1979, a pair of Prairie Falcons used the ledge to lay four eggs. Two young birds fledged from the site.

Prairie Falcons have also been known to nest on artificial structures such as windmill stones, shepherd's monuments (small rock pillars), and other types of towers when nest sites are not available in cliffs. These substrates are generally not effective, because they lack a nest platform. If another bird has abandoned a nest and created a platform of sticks, Prairie Falcons have taken over and bred successfully. In higher-elevation eyries in Oregon, the only suitable nesting platforms that Prairie Falcons could find were Ravens' abandoned stick nests.

In Nevada, a pair of Prairie Falcons also used a Ravens' nest. In 1985, the birds were found on the tower of a 345-kv transmission line, where Ravens had previously built a stick nest. Observers counted five eggs, which produced young birds that fledged. A second nest along the same transmission line was found in 1986.

Adult falcon equipped with a solar transmitter used to study falcon movements and migration. *Photo by Rick Kline*

Human impacts on Prairie Falcon populations can be severe; however, as development occurs we can introduce a number of mitigative measures to enhance the populations of these magnificent birds. By controlling access to nesting areas during the critical nesting and fledging periods, and by limiting blasting and other noisy activities during these times, young birds can grow and fledge into healthy adults. If eyries are destroyed, they can be re-created to attract the birds. In fact, if the prey base is adequate, we can attract Prairie Falcons to new areas by constructing nest and perch sites. Finally, we must preserve the birds' prey base so that they can find adequate food for themselves and their young.

V

WHERE DO WE GO FROM HERE?

There is still much we do not know about how to effectively manage and maintain this beautiful, popular bird in the western United States. We still do not know exactly how disturbance affects Prairie Falcons. For instance, we do know that when extensive development occurs in an area, such as mining or construction, the birds do not return. But we could attribute this to a reduction in the prey base or simply to the birds' intolerance of people for long periods of time. We need to know how much disturbance the bird can withstand and, more precisely, how the disturbance affects the bird.

Historically, there have been a number of studies on the movement patterns of Prairie Falcons. But a number of unanswered questions remain: How do the young birds disperse? and Where do they go? In addition, we know very little about their winter movements, and their entire winter ecology is largely unknown. There have been some studies involving banded birds. Banded birds allow us to see if birds return to occupy the same sites, but recovery of banded birds is difficult because it is hard to find carcasses. Radio telemetry, including the use of satellites, can allow biologists to understand movement and mortality factors of the Prairie Falcon. Whereas earlier literature indicates that the birds paired for life, later data shows that this occurs only in some cases. This means that we need to know where the male and female move seasonally to better understand Prairie Falcon nesting and reproduction.

While we examine movement patterns, we also need to understand quite a number of behavioral patterns in order to better manage this falcon. The timing of copulation and of nesting are both important factors that might be affected by human disturbance, including disruption by birdwatchers. Once such patterns are understood, then we could provide improved guidelines on how to manage the bird.

The long-term population trends of Prairie Falcons seem to be most affected by human disturbance, habitat loss, and, in some cases, indiscriminate shooting of the birds. In order to understand these long-term population trends, we need to be able to collect data over many years. Indeed, if we only look for a short time, we may be examining a fluctuation or a short-term change in a population. Fluctuations occur annually in many populations. Raptors are long-lived birds that are influenced by weather conditions. For example, Squires found that a heavy snowstorm in north-central Wyoming prevented all Prairie Falcons in the Pumpkin Buttes area from successfully raising nestlings that year. These harsh spring storms that come through some of the areas where Prairie Falcons nest can, indeed, hinder production for one year and result in population fluctuations. Long-term trends, however, are not apparent from these changes.

The impacts of disturbances to Prairie Falcon habitat need to be addressed. How habitat fragmentation affects nesting birds and their use of a foraging area is important to know as we develop some remote areas. We do not know to what degree heavy grazing affects the birds' prey base. Conversion of native prairie to agricultural lands may also have an impact on the birds, particularly on their prey base.

Currently, a number of genetic studies are underway on different wildlife species. Prairie Falcons are being karyotyped—that is, researchers are examining the birds' chromosomes and genetic material. Initial studies on karyotypes of Peregrine, Prairie, and Gyrfalcons have been reported, and the results show that the Peregrine and Prairie Falcon karyotypes appear to be almost identical, whereas the Gyrfalcon has two additional pairs of chromosomes and appears to have a karyotype similar to the Lanner. This indicates a very close relationship between the Prairie and Peregrine Falcon. It also implies that the male hybrid of the Peregrine and Prairie Falcon could be fertile. In all likelihood, therefore, behavior patterns are isolating the birds, if these data are correct. Additional investigations can make a contribution by determining genetic relationships of birds, which may assist us in the overall management of the different species. Captive-breeding studies will also be most useful, since we may be able to replenish areas where birds have been lost or displaced by human activities such as hunting. As we move into the next century, we need to keep in mind that humans create the greatest disturbance of the Prairie Falcon. We need more and continued efforts to reduce harmful impacts on this beautiful bird.

Sources

I. FALCONRY

Falconry: Cade 1982; Newton 1990; Hoskings and Hoskings 1987; Grossman and Hamlet 1964; Peterson 1948; Kenward 1979.
Training Prairie Falcon: Haak 1992.

II. CAPTIVE BREEDING

Captive Breeding: Waller 1962; Cade, Weaver, Platt, and Burham 1977; Burnham 1983; Parks and Hardaswick 1987; Boyd, Boyd, and Dooler 1977; Granger 1977.

III. PESTICIDES

Types of Pesticides: Anderson, Beiswinger, and Purdom 1993; Ogden and Hornocker 1977.

Prairie Falcons and Pesticides: Nelson 1969; Fyfe, Campbell, Hayson, and Hodson 1969; Enderson and Berger 1970; Garrett and Mitchell 1973; Boyce Jr. 1985; Squires 1986.

IV. HABITAT MITIGATION

Habitat Mitigation: Denton 1975; Squires, Anderson, and Oakleaf 1993; Bedbarz 1984; Holthuijzen 1990; Fyfe and Olendorff 1976; Harmata, Durr, and Geduldig 1978; Boyce, Fisher, and Peterson 1980; Fyfe and Armbruster 1977; Runde 1987; Haak 1995; Roppe, Siegel, and Wilder 1989.

V. WHERE DO WE GO FROM HERE?

Where Do We Go from Here?: Fyfe, Campbell, Hayson, and Hodson 1969; Schmutz and Oliphant 1987.

CHAPTER 5

Conclusion

*W*atching Prairie Falcons brings back many memories of our experiences with the species. One spring morning about 5:00 A.M., we were trapping two adults in order to attach radio transmitters. Telemetry was necessary for us to study habitat-use preferences. We placed a live lure owl at the cliff base below the eyrie and protected the owl with two net panels. Nets break away when struck at high speeds and prevent injury to the falcon. Soon the female spotted the owl and began "cacking" as she flew above the trap. She plunged down vertically directly at the owl but pulled up just in time to only tip the net with her foot. The net broke away from the trap pole and ensnared her foot, but she was still able to fly. To our horror, the falcon was flying in high, wide circles above her eyrie, the net streaming out behind. She looked like an airplane pulling an advertisement banner. We felt helpless knowing that she would become entangled and die as soon as she landed on a cliff or tree. We also remember our total relief as we watched the net suddenly break away from the bird and parachute harmlessly to the ground. We captured the falcon without incident the following day.

The Prairie Falcon is truly the premier falcon of the West. Many populations appear stable, and their abundance makes them the most accessible large falcon to all people. Falconers, who appreciate their speed, endurance, and incredible courage when hunting, marvel at their ability to capture prey. Trained Prairie Falcons have entertained thousands of football fans, as when falconers from the U.S. Air Force Academy fly their birds during halftime shows. Unfortunately for the Academy, when its team plays the University of Wyoming football team at Laramie, the Prairie Falcons sometimes have their own ideas during the shows. When the falcons soar high over the stadium and see the wide-open prairie, they have at times ignored the frenetic antics of the falconers below and set their wings for the wide-open country, never to be seen again.

Interest in watching captive falcons is limited; most people get excited about watching wild Prairie Falcons as they patrol the cliff faces that protect their eyries. Raptor enthusiasts want to experience firsthand the thrill of a large falcon diving inches from their heads. People who appreciate the forces that shaped the evolution of both predator and prey enjoy watching Prairie Falcons hunt their quarry. Some flights are as thrilling as observing a hunting falcon plummet through a flock of Mallards; other flights consist merely of a falcon gliding from a utility pole to pounce on a field mouse. During the winter, bird watchers can readily observe Prairie Falcons hunting horned larks on agricultural lands throughout the Great Plains.

The most important thing that people should remember when enjoying Prairie Falcons is how inextricably linked they are to their prey. The prairie ecosystem needs to be considered holistically; Prairie Falcons are just one part of the whole. Prairie Falcons, along with Golden Eagles, Ferruginous Hawks, and Coyotes, are top-level carnivores in the food chain of the prairie ecosystem. During nesting, the Prairie Falcons' entire activity pattern is influenced by the birds and small mammals that comprise their diet. The abundance and distribution of prey determine the habitats that falcons hunt. Life-history patterns of prey also affect dispersal patterns of fledglings. For instance, young birds may disperse over vast distances in search of food when ground squirrels estivate in late summer, or they may remain nearer their natal territory if food remains abundant. During the winter, Prairie Falcons migrate to agricultural lands on the eastern plains in search of prey, especially horned larks.

Thus, habitat requirements of many Prairie Falcon populations change drastically from winter to summer. Whether foraging on agricultural lands during the winter or depending on undisturbed sagebrush steppe-grasslands during nesting, they must often shift from primarily avian prey during the winter to

Prairie Falcon cliff and hunting habitat. *Photo by LuRay Parker, Wyoming Game and Fish Department*

mammalian prey during nesting. Conserving the species requires that we consider habitat requirements throughout all seasons.

Another memory we treasure involves a rancher who owned several cliffs that were used by nesting Prairie Falcons. We had researched this falcon population for several years, and local ranchers were interested in our work. Many ranchers were possessive of "their" falcons and enjoyed watching them as they worked the cattle.

We were banding young falcons, and a rancher named John asked to come along. We drove up to the spot were the cliff dropped off 150 feet to the prairie below. A Prairie Falcon that nested on this cliff spotted us and began diving and "cacking"

Falcon perched on cliff. *Photo by Rick Kline*

to defend her nest. John is a tall man—about 6'3". He wore cowboy boots even for rock climbing. He had watched Prairie Falcons all his life but had never seen an eyrie up close. John also had never rappelled, but he still wanted to see "his" falcons. I tried to convince him to tie on a second rope as a safety line; he declined. In a classic display of western machismo he said, "I ain't scared or nothing, if that's what you mean."

John backed over the cliff without a pause and kept slipping rope through his hands. The problem was he would not move his feet; they were frozen in place. From our vantage point, we could no longer see his head. We could only see the soles of his cowboy boots pointing straight up at the sky. The sound of rope slipping through carabiners then stopped; all was quiet.

Now the toes of his boots were starting to point out away from the cliff; things were not going well. We peered over the edge of the cliff and found John hanging almost completely upside down. He was gripping the rope with both hands and looked up at us a little wild-eyed between his feet, which had not moved since he began climbing.

"Scared yet?" we asked. Nodding his head frantically, he said, "Yea, I'm plenty scared!" We convinced him to begin shuffling his feet down so that his body hung horizontal to the cliff. We lowered him a safety line. After regaining his composure, he began rappelling down the cliff like an ex-Marine. The cliff began jetting inward, forming a large overhang that protected the eyrie. John's feet could no longer touch the cliff, and he began slowly spinning as he descended in a free rappel. When he reached the eyrie, he was whooping and hollering in true cowboy style while both adult falcons were swooping inches from his head. The three chicks calmly watched his antics from the safety of their eyrie. John was quite fired up by the time he reached the ground. That day, Prairie Falcons left an impression on him that his grandchildren will hear about.

Currently, most Prairie Falcon populations appear stable, but their fate is tied to the future of western rangelands. Land-use changes such as urbanization, conversion of native rangelands to agriculture, and energy development, with its accompanying increase in human disturbance, can devastate falcon populations. Wildlife once common on rangelands, such as Northern Shrikes and Ferruginous Hawks, may already be declining. Prairie Falcon populations will become increasingly vulnerable as disturbances to native rangelands continue.

Biologists know very little about the prairie ecosystem. We do not understand how forces such as habitat fragmentation affect the abundance and persistence of prey populations. We believe that humans, like Prairie Falcons, need open space to thrive. Our grandchildren's opportunity to watch this magnificent falcon depends on our commitment today to managing and preserving native rangelands.

Raptor Etiquette

*B*irds of prey are among the most fascinating members of the avian world. Audiences watching captive raptors are often spellbound by the opportunity of seeing these birds up close. In the same way, being at a wild raptor's nest is an exciting experience, because the adults and young hatchlings are easily observed.

When we become completely absorbed watching an attacking falcon scream and dive at us while we are near a nest, it is easy to lose track of time entirely. During this period of infatuation, we may inadvertently keep the adult off the nest for too long, and the eggs or small nestlings may be harmed. Therefore, it is critically important that we act responsibly around raptors so that our actions are not responsible for failed nesting attempts. Getting that "one last look" or insisting on a full-frame photograph may be accomplished at the birds' expense. We are the visitors when touring the nesting territories of raptors. Their continued well-being must be the litmus by which we evaluate our actions.

Acting responsibly around nesting raptors mainly involves good common sense and compassion for the birds' well-being. However, some potential problems are not obvious and should be considered before venturing afield to look for falcons. Fyfe and Olendorff have identified several potential problems that may be caused by visiting raptor nests:

(1) *Parents becoming so disturbed they desert their eggs or young*

How birds will react to disturbance of their nesting site cannot be predicted. The response depends on the species of raptor, nest-site characteristics, the personality of the individual bird, and the duration and intensity of the disturbance. The falcons' reaction to intruders also depends on the stage of their nesting cycle. Falcons are most susceptible to disturbance during early spring, when the female spends much time sitting on or near her empty nest. At this time, Prairie Falcons and Peregrines have deserted their nest sites (both before and during egg laying and incubation) after a single intrusion by a human. Therefore, Prairie Falcons should not be disturbed during early spring

(April through early May in Wyoming). When young are present, desertion is unlikely.

(2) *Damage to eggs and young by frightened adults*

If raptors are suddenly frightened and leave the nest site in a panic, they can inadvertently crush or puncture eggs or can eject eggs or young from the nest in their excitement. It is only natural for a person eager to observe a nesting raptor closely to approach the nest site very quietly. However, the raptor may not notice you until you are quite close; this causes the bird to burst out of the nest site, possibly destroying or catapulting the eggs or young. It is far better to let the bird know you are approaching the nest site by making noises, such as clapping, singing, and whistling, or to advance toward the nest in the line of sight. The noise should be slight at first, then become progressively louder when nearing the nest, until the adult leaves the eyrie. The bird then becomes aware of your presence before you are perceived to be an extreme threat.

Prairie Falcons often place their feet underneath the eggs when incubating or straddle young nestlings when brooding. By giving warning of your approach, the falcon can carefully remove her feet from under the eggs or can calmly bypass young when leaving the eyrie. During the actual hatch, Prairie Falcons are very reluctant to leave the eyrie. Therefore, if the bird does not fly, it is best to immediately leave the area and not return to the eyrie until the young are midsized nestlings—approximately ten days to two weeks of age.

(3) *Cooling, overheating, and loss of moisture to eggs*

Egg cooling is usually not a problem if your visit is less than ten minutes. However, in the dry, hot areas of the western United States, where Prairie Falcons typically nest, overheating from direct sunlight can be a serious problem. Also, unattended eggs in dry air and sunlight do not have the normal moisture transfer from the female's brood patch, which may cause dehydration of the eggs that is extremely detrimental to their hatching. Most Prairie Falcon eyries are in potholes and are protected from direct sun, but falcons often nest on old eagle nests which offer little shading. Eggs placed in "pothole" eyries may even be vulnerable to direct sun, depending on sun position and the exposure of the eyrie. The best rule is to keep all visits short (under ten minutes) when the nest contains eggs. It is even more important to avoid visiting any raptor nest during the egg stage and to wait until after hatching, when disturbance is less of a problem.

(4) *Chill and heat prostration of nestlings*

Young nestlings are more susceptible to overheating than excessive cooling. Except when temperatures are below 45° F, young birds will be fine during short visits. However, young hatchling Prairie Falcons exposed to direct sun can be killed in short order. Parent birds shade their young with outstretched wings to offer protection from over-heating. When the parent is flushed from her eyrie during a visit, no protection from the sun is available, making the young vulnerable. Young Prairie Falcons are much less susceptible to overheating after they are at least 2.5 weeks of age.

(5) *Premature fledging*

Late in the nesting cycle, young falcons often sit near the edge of the eyrie, flapping and exercising their wings. They are unable to fly at this stage but are still able hop about the cliff face from perch to perch. If a person suddenly peers over the cliff's edge, the panicked falcons may dive from the cliff even though flightless; the young birds may break legs or wings, or may be killed outright from the impact of the fall. It is important the young falcons know you are approaching, so making noise before encountering the birds is advisable. In all cases, approaching birds just before fledging is risky and is seldom justified. If a young falcon is accidentally flushed from the eyrie, you should carefully note where the falcon lands. After capturing and inspecting the young bird for injury, return it as close to the eyrie as possible without causing the remaining young birds to scatter.

It is an incredibly exciting experience to stand near a Prairie Falcon eyrie, listening to their calls and watching the adults dive within a few feet of our heads. We all leave such experiences with renewed fascination for these wondrous birds. However, our actions as falcon admirers must never compromise the productivity of nesting pairs or the safety of their hatchlings. If we act responsibly when observing falcon eyries and are aware of ways to minimize our potential impact, we can still experience the wonders of watching nesting Prairie Falcons, without endangering their productivity.

Literature Cited

A.O.U. 1983. Check-list of North American birds. American Ornithologists' Union. Allen Press, Lawrence, Kansas.

Allen, G. T. 1987. Estimating prairie falcon and golden eagle nesting populations in North Dakota. Journal of Wildlife Management 51: 739–744.

Allen, G. T., R. K. Murphy, and K. Steenhof. 1986. Late fledging dates, renesting, and large clutches of prairie falcons. Wilson Bulletin 98:463–465.

Amadon, D. 1975. Why are female birds of prey larger than males? Raptor Research 9:1–11.

Andersen, D. E. 1988. Common barn-owl killed by a prairie falcon. Southwestern Naturalist 33:377–378.

Anderson, S. H., R. E. Beiswinger, and D. W. Purdom. 1993. Environmental Science. Macmillan, New York.

Ankney, C. D., and D. M. Scott. 1980. Changes in nutrient reserves and diet of breeding brown-headed cowbirds. Auk 97:684–696.

Bailey, A. M., and R. J. Niedrach. 1933. The prairie falcon. American Forests 39:356–358, 384.

Balgooyen, T. G. 1976. Behavior and ecology of the American kestrel (*Falco sparverius* L.). University of California Publications in Zoology 103:1–85.

Balgooyen, T. G. 1988. A unique encounter among a gyrfalcon, peregrine falcon, prairie falcon, and American kestrel. Journal of Raptor Research 22:71.

Bammann, A. R., and J. H. Doremus. 1982. The Snake River Birds of Prey Study Area bird list. Department of the Interior, B.L.M., Boise, Idaho.

Beasom, S. L., and O. H. Patte. 1978. Utilization of snails by Rio Grande turkey hens. Journal of Wildlife Management 42:916–919.

Beauvais, G., J. H. Enderson, and A. J. Magro. 1992. Home range, habitat use and behavior of prairie falcons wintering in east-central Colorado. Journal of Raptor Research 26(1):13–18.

Becker, D. M. 1979. A survey of raptors on national forest land in Carter County, Montana. U.S. Forest Service, Northern Region. Final Report (unpublished). 61 pp.

Bednarz, J. C. 1984. The effect of mining and blasting on breeding prairie falcon occupancy in the Caballo Mountains, New Mexico. Raptor Research 18:16–19.

Beebe, F. L. 1960. The marine peregrine of the north west Pacific coast. Condor 62:145–189.

Bent, A. C. 1937. Life histories of North American birds of prey, order falconiformes. Part 1. United States National Museum Bulletin 167. Dover Publications, New York.

Birkhead, T. R., L. Atkin, and A. P. Moller. 1987. Copulation behavior of birds. Behaviour 100:103–138.

Birkhead, T. R,. and C. M. Lessells. 1988. Copulation behavior of the osprey, *Pandion Haliaetus.* Animal Behavior 36:1672–1682.

Bond, R. M. 1936. Some observations on the food of prairie falcons. The Condor 38:169–170.

Boyce, D. A., Jr. 1985. Prairie falcon prey in the Mojave Desert, California. Raptor Research 19:128–134.

Boyce, D. A., Jr., R. L. Garrett, and B. J. Walton. 1986. Distribution and density of prairie falcons nesting in California during the 1970s. Raptor Research 20:71–74.

Boyce, D.A., L. Fisher, and J. Peterson. 1980. Prairie falcon nest on an artificial cliff. Raptor Research 14:46–50.

Boyd, L. L., N. S. Boyd, and F. C. Dooler. 1977. Reproduction of prairie falcon by artificial insemination. Journal of Wildlife Management 41:266–271.

Braun, C. E., J. E. Enderson, C. J. Henny, H. Meng, and A. G. Nye, Jr. 1977. Falconry effects on raptor populations and management in North America. Wilson Bulletin 89:310–369.

Brown, L. H., and D. Amadon. 1968. Eagles, hawks, and falcons of the world. Country Life Books, Hamlyn Publishing Group, Hamlyn House, Feltham, Middlesex, Great Britain.

Burnham, W. A. 1983. Artificial incubation of falcon eggs. Journal of Wildlife Management 47:158–168.

Cade, T. 1982. The falcons of the world. Cornell University Press, Ithaca, New York. 183 pp.

Cade, T. J., J. D. Weaver, J. B. Platt, and W. A. Burham. 1977. The propagation of large falcons in captivity. Raptor Research 11:28–48.

Cade, T. L. 1960. Ecology of the peregrine and gyrfalcon in Alaska. University of California Publications in Zoology 63:151–200.

Call, M. 1979. Habitat management guide for birds of prey. U.S. Bureau of Land Management. Denver, Colorado. Technical Note 6611. 70 pp.

Clark, W. S., and B. K. Wheeler. 1987. A field guide to hawks, North America. Houghton Mifflin, Boston. 198 pp.

Clark, W. S., M. E. Pramstaller, and B. Pratt. 1980. Field I.D. guide for North American raptors. Raptor Information Center, National Wildlife Federation.

Cave, A. J. 1968. The breeding of the kestrel, *Falco tinnunculus* L., in the reclaimed area Oostelijk Flevoland, Netherlands. Journal of Zoology 18:313–407.

Conway, C. J., D. E. Runde, D. Abbite, and S. H. Anderson. 1993. Effects of a long-term experimental harvest on prairie falcon in southwestern Wyoming (1982–1989). Wyoming Cooperative Fish and Wildlife Research Unit, Laramie, Wyoming. 40 pp.

Craig, T. H., and E. H. Craig. 1984. Results of a helicopter survey of cliff nesting raptors in a deep canyon in southern Idaho. Raptor Research 18:20–25.

Cramp, S., et al., eds. 1980. Handbook of the birds of Europe, the Middle East and North Africa. The birds of the western Palearctic. Volume II: Hawks to Bustards. Oxford University Press, London. 277 pp.

Darwin, C. 1871. The descent of man and selection in relation to sex. John Murray, London.

Dekker, D. 1982. Occurrence and foraging habits of prairie falcons, *Falco mexicanus,* at Beaverhill Lake, Alberta. Canadian Field-Naturalist 96:477–478.

Denton, S. J. 1975. Status of the prairie falcon breeding in Oregon. M.S. thesis. Oregon State University, Corvalis.

DiDonato, J. E. 1992. Intra specific nest defense by prairie falcons. Journal of Raptor Research 26:40.

Edwards, B. F. 1973. A nesting study of a small pululation of prairie falcons in southern Alberta. Canadian Field-Naturalist 87:322–324.

Ellis, D. H., and D. L. Groat. 1982. A prairie falcon fledgling intrudes at a peregrine falcon eyrie and pirates prey. Raptor Research 16:89–90.

Enderson, J. H. 1962. Ecology of the prairie falcon (*Falco mexicanus*) in the central Rocky Mountain region. Ph.D. dissertation. University of Wyoming, Laramie. 87 pp.

Enderson, J. H. 1964. A study of the prairie falcon in the central Rocky Mountain region. Auk 81:332–352.

Enderson, J. H., and D. D. Berger. 1970. Pesticides: eggshell thinning and lowered production of young in prairie falcons. Bioscience 20:355–356.

Enderson, J. H., S. A. Temple, and L. G. Swartz. 1973. Time lapse photographic records of nesting peregrine falcons. Living Birds 11:113–128.

Fisher, A. K. 1883. Hawks and owls of the United States in their relation to agriculture. U. S. Dept. of Agriculture Bulletin 3. U.S. Government Printing Office, Washington, D.C.

Fox, N. 1977. The biology of the New Zealand Falcon. Ph.D. dissertation. University of Kent, Canterbury, England.

Fyfe, R. 1972. Breeding behavior of captive and wild prairie and peregrine falcons. Raptor Research 6 (Supp. C):43–52.

Fyfe, R. W., and H. I. Armbruster. 1977. Raptor research and management in Canada. In R.D. Chancellor, ed., World conference on birds of prey: report of proceedings, pp. 282–293. International Council for Bird Preservation, Vienna, Austria.

Fyfe, R. W., J. Campbell, B. Hayson, and K. Hodson. 1969. Regional population declines and organo-chlorine insecticides in Canadian prairie falcons. Canadian Field-Naturalist 83:191–200.

Fyfe, R. W., and R. R. Olendorff. 1976. Minimizing the dangers of nesting studies to raptors and other sensitive species. Canadian Wildlife Service Occasional Paper No. 23. 17 pp.

Garrett, R. L., and D. J. Mitchell. 1973. A study of prairie falcon populations in California. California Department of Fish and Game. Wildlife Management Branch Administrative Report No. 73–2 (unpublished). 15 pp.

Gillespie, M. M. 1981. Prairie falcon harasses Canada goose. Blue Jay 39:109.

Goss, N. S. 1991. History of the birds of Kansas. George W. Crane, Topeka.

Granger, S. E. 1977. Reintroduction of captive-bred prairie falcons in California. Raptor Research 11:73.

Greenwood, P. J. 1980. Mating systems, philopatry and dispersal in birds and mammals. Animal Behavior 28:1140–1162.

Grossman, M. L., and J. Hamlet. 1964. Birds of prey of the world. Bonanza Books, New York.

Haak, B. A. 1982. Foraging ecology of prairie falcons in northern California. M.S. thesis. Oregon State University, Corvallis. 64 pp.

Haak, B. A. 1992. The hunting falcon. Hancock House Publishers, Blaine, Washington. 239 pp.

Haak, B. A. 1995. Pirate of the Plains. Adventures with Prairie Falcon in the high desert. Hancock House Publishers, Blaine, Washington.

Harmata, A. R., J. E. Durr, and H. Geduldig. 1978. Home range, activity patterns and habitat use of prairie falcons nesting in the Mojave Desert. 89 pp. Prepared by Colorado Wildlife Services, Fort Collins, Colo., for the U.S. Bureau of Land Management, Riverside, California.

Heintzelman, D. S. 1979. A guide to hawk watching in North America. Keystone Books, Pennsylvania State University Press, University Park, Pennsylvania. 284 pp.

Hickey, J. J. 1942. Eastern populations of the duck hawk. Auk 59: 176–204.

Holthuijzen, A. M. A. 1990. Prey delivery, caching, and retrieval rates in nesting prairie falcons. The Condor 92:475–484.

Holthuijzen A. M. A. 1992. Frequency and timing of copulations in the prairie falcon. Wilson Bulletin 104:333–338.

Holthuijzen, A. M. A., and W. G. Eastland. 1985. Responses of breeding prairie falcons (*Falco mexicanus*) to experimental blasting. p. 9 (Abstract only). In Raptor Research Foundation Symposium on the Management of Birds of Prey. International Meeting. Session 10. Second Raptor Research Foundation Conference on Raptor Conservation Techniques. Lawrence, Kansas.

Holthuijzen, A. M. A., P. A. Duley, J. C. Hager, S. A. Smith, and K. N. Wood. 1987. Piracy, insectivory and cannibalism of prairie falcons (*Falco mexicanus*) nesting in southwestern Idaho. Journal of Raptor Research 21(1):32–33.

Hoskings, E., and D. Hoskings. 1987. Birds of prey of the world. Stephen Greene Press, Lexington, Massachusetts.

Johnsgard, P. A. 1990. Hawks, eagles, and falcons of North America: Biology and natural history. Smithsonian Institution Press, London. 403 pp.

Kenward, R. 1979. The numbers of birds of prey obtained and possessed by falconers in the United Kingdom. The Falconer 7:158–163.

Kocan, A. A., and L. R. Gordon. 1976. Fatal air sac infection with *Serratospiculum amaculata* in a prairie falcon. Journal of the American Veterinary Medical Association 169:908.

Krapu, G. L., and Swanson, G. A. 1975. Some nutritional aspects of reproduction in prairie nesting pintails. Journal of Wildlife Management 39:156–162.

Lanning, D. V., and M. A. Hitchcock. 1991. Breeding distribution and habitat of prairie falcons in northern Mexico. The Condor 93: 762–765.

Leedy, R. R. 1972. The status of prairie falcons in western Montana: Special emphasis on possible effects of chlorinated hydrocarbon insecticides. M.S. thesis. University of Montana, Missoula. 96 pp.

MacLaren, P. A., S. H. Anderson, and D. E. Runde. 1988. Food habits and nest characteristics of breeding raptors in southwestern Wyoming. Great Basin Naturalist 48:548–553.

Marti, C. D., and C. E. Braun. 1975. Use of tundra habitats by prairie falcons in Colorado. The Condor 77:213–214.

Marzluff, J. M., B. A. Kimsey, L. S. Schueck, M. McFadzen, M. S. Vekasy, and J. C. Bednarz. 1996. The influence of habitat, prey abundance, sex, and breeding success on the ranging habits and habitat selection of prairie falcons. (in press)

McFadzen, M. E., and J. M. Marzluff. 1996. Behavior of prairie falcons during the nesting and fledgling-dependence periods under fluctuating prey conditions. (in press)

McLaren, P. A., D. E. Runde, and S. H. Anderson. 1984. A record of tree-nesting prairie falcons in Wyoming. Condor 86:487–488.

Mead, C. J. 1973. Cited in Newton, I., 1979. Population ecology of raptors. Buteo Books, Vermillion, South Dakota.

Mearns, R., and I. Newton. 1984. Turnover and dispersal in a peregrine *Falco peregrinus* population. Ibis 126:347–355.

Merchant, S. S. 1982. A possible hunting relationship between two raptor species. Raptor Research 16:26–27.

Moller, A. P. 1987. Copulation behavior in the goshawk, *Accipiter gentilis*. Animal Behavior 35:755–763.

Moore, T. D., L. E. Spence, and C. E. Dugnolle. 1974. Identification of the dorsal guard hairs of some mammals of Wyoming. Wyoming Game and Fish Department Bulletin 14. 177 pp.

Moritisch, M. 1983. Photographic guide for aging nestling prairie falcons. U.S. Department of Interior, Bureau of Land Management. Snake River Birds of Prey Project, Boise, Idaho.

Morrison, M. L., and B. J. Walton. 1980. The laying of replacement clutches by falconiformes and strigiformes in North America. Raptor Research 4:79–85.

Morton, M. L., and P. W. Sherman. 1978. Effects of a spring snowstorm on behavior, reproduction, and survival of Belding's ground squirrels. Canadian Journal of Zoology 56:2578–2590.

Mueller, H. C., and K. Meyer. 1985. The evolution of reversed sexual dimorphism in size: A comparative analysis of the Falconiformes of the western Palearctic. In R. F. Johnston, ed., Current Ornithology, Vol. 2, pp. 65–101.

Murie, J. O., and G. R. Michener. 1984. The biology of ground-dwelling squirrels. University of Nebraska Press, Lincoln. 459 pp.

Nelson, M. W. 1969. States of the peregrine falcon in the Northwest. Chapter 4 in J. J. Hickey, ed., Peregrine Falcon Populations: Their Biological Decline. University of Wisconsin Press, Madison. 596 pp.

Newton, I. 1979. Population ecology of raptors. Buteo Books. Vermillion, South Dakota. 399 pp.

Newton, I., ed. 1990. Birds of prey. Facts on File, New York.

Newton, I., and M. Marquiss. 1983. Dispersal of sparrowhawks between birthplace and breeding place. Journal of Animal Ecology 52:463–477.

Oakleaf, R. 1985. Raptor research and management in Wyoming. Eyas 8:18–21.

Ogden, V. T. 1973. Nesting density and reproductive success of the prairie falcon in Southwestern Idaho. M.S. thesis. University of Idaho, Moscow.

Ogden, V. T. 1975. Nesting density and reproductive success of the prairie falcon in southwest Idaho. In J. R. Murphy, C. M. White, and B. E. Harrell. Proceedings of the Conference on Raptor Conservation and Telemetry. Raptor Research Report #3, Raptor Research Foundation, Vermillion, South Dakota.

Ogden, V. T., and M. G. Hornocker. 1977. Nesting density and success of prairie falcons in southwestern Idaho. Journal of Wildlife Management 41:1–11.

Olendorff, R. P., and J. W. Stoddard. 1974. The potential for management of raptor populations in western grasslands. Raptor Research Report 2:47–88.

Olendorff, R. P., R. S. Motioni, and M. W. Call. 1980. Raptor management: The state of the art in 1980. U.S. Bureau of Land Management, Denver, Colorado. Technical Note 345. 56 pp.

Parks, J. E., and V. Hardaswick. 1987. Fertility and hatchability of falcon eggs after insemination with frozen peregrine falcon semen. Journal of Raptor Research 21:70–72.

Peterson, R. T. 1948. Birds of prey. Facts on File, New York.

Platt, S. W. 1975. The Mexican chicken bug as a source of raptor mortality. Wilson Bulletin 87:557.

Platt, S. W. 1977. Successful breeding of juvenile prairie falcons in northeast Colorado. Raptor Research 11(4):81–82.

Platte, S. W. 1981. Prairie falcon: Aspects of population dynamics, individual vocal identification, marking and sexual maturity. Ph.D. dissertation. Brigham Young University, Salt Lake City. 91 pp.

Porter, R. D., and C. M. White. 1973. The peregrine falcon in Utah emphasizing ecology and competition with the prairie falcon. Brigham Young University Science Bulletin Biological Service 18(1):1–74.

Richards, G. L. 1965. Prairie falcon imitates flight patterns of loggerhead shrike. Great Basin Naturalist 25:48.

Richardson, F. 1972. Accessory pygostyle bones of *Falconidae*. Condor 74:350–351.

Roppe, J. A., S. M. Siegel, and S. E. Wilder. 1989. Prairie falcon nesting on transmission towers. Condor 91:711–712.

Runde, D. E. 1987. Population dynamics, habitat use and movement patterns of the prairie falcon (*Falco Mexicanus*). Ph.D. dissertation. University of Wyoming, Laramie. 166 pp.

Runde, D. E., and S. A. Anderson. 1986. Characteristics of cliff and nest sites used by breeding prairie falcons. Raptor Research 20:21–28.

Savile, D. B. O. 1957. Adaptive evolution in the avian wing. Evolution 11:212–224.

Schmutz, S. M., and L. W. Oliphant. 1987. Chromosome study of peregrine, prairie and gyrfalcons with implications for hybrids. Journal of Heredity 78:388–390.

Sherrod, S. K. 1978. Diets of North American falconiformes. Raptor Research 12:49–121.

Sitter, G. 1983. Feeding activity and behavior of prairie falcons in the Snake River Birds of Prey Natural Area in southwestern Idaho. M.S. thesis. University of Idaho, Boise. 64 pp.

Skinner, M. P. 1938. Prairie Falcon. In A. C. Bent, Life histories of North American birds of prey, pp. 18–22. U. S. National Museum Bulletin 167.

Smith, D. G., and J. R. Murphy. 1973. Breeding ecology of raptors in the eastern Great Basin of Utah. Brigham Young University Science Bulletin., Biological Service, vol. 28(3).

Smith, E. D. 1985. Construction of artificial nesting sites for prairie falcons. Wildlife Society Bulletin 13:543–546.

Snow, C. 1974. Habitat management series for unique or endangered species. Report No. 8. Prairie falcon *Falco mexicanus*. U.S. Department of the Interior, Bureau of Land Management. Technical Note. ii + 18 pp.

Sodhi, N. S. 1991. Pair copulations, extra-air copulations, and intra-specific nest intrusions in merlin. The Condor 93:433–437.

Squires, J. R. 1986. Productivity, movement and food habits of prairie falcons in Campbell County, Wyoming. M.S. thesis. University of Wyoming, Laramie. 189 pp.

Squires, J. R., S. H. Anderson, and R. Oakleaf. 1989. Food habits of nesting prairie falcons in Campbell County, Wyoming. Journal of Raptor Research 23:157–161.

Squires, J., S. H. Anderson, and R. Oakleaf. 1991. Prairie falcons quit nesting in response to spring snowstorm. Journal of Field Ornithology 62:191–194.

Squires, J., S. H. Anderson, and R. Oakleaf. 1993. Home range size and habitat-use patterns of nesting prairie falcons, near oil developments in northeastern Wyoming. Journal of Field Ornithology. 64:1–10.

Steenhof, K., and M. N. Kochert. 1988. Dietary responses of three raptor species to changing prey densities in a natural environment. Journal of Animal Ecology 57:37–48.

Steenhof, K., M. N. Kochert, and M. Q. Moritsch. 1984. Dispersal and migration of southwestern Idaho raptors. Journal of Field Ornithology 55:357–368.

Thompson, B. C., and J. E. Tabor. 1981. Mallard using moving vehicles for predator avoidance. Wilson Bulletin 93:277–278.

Tyler, J. G. 1923. Observations of the habits of the prairie falcon. Condor 25:90–97.

U.S. Department of the Interior. 1979. Snake River Birds of Prey special research report to the Secretary of Interior. Bureau of Land Management, Boise, Idaho. 142 pp.

Waller, R. 1962. Der Wilde Falistmein Gesell. Verl. Nermann-Neudamm, Mekungen.

Walton, B. S. 1977. Development of techniques for raptor management, with emphasis on the peregrine falcon. California Fish and Game Report No. 77–4.

Webster, H. M., Jr. 1944. A survey of the prairie falcon in Colorado. Auk 61:609–616.

White, C. M. 1962. Prairie falcon displays accipitrine and circinine hunting methods. The Condor 64:439–440.

White, C. M., and D. G. Roseneau. 1970. Observations on food, nesting and winter populations of large North American falcons. The Condor 72:113–115.

Williams, R., and C. P. Matteson, Jr. 1947. Wyoming hawks. Wyoming Wildlife 11:20–28.

Williams, R. N. 1985. Relationships between prairie falcon nesting phenology, latitude and elevation. Raptor Research 19:139–142.

Wrege, P. H., and T. J. Cade 1977. Courtship behavior of large falcons in captivity. Raptor Research 11:1–27.

Ydenberg, R. C., and L. S. Forbes. 1991. The survival-reproduction selection equilibrium and reversed size dimorphism in raptors. Oikos 60:115–119.

Index

Accipiter (forest hawks), 88, 89
Accipitridae, 87, 100, 101
aldrin, 123
American Kestrel, 29, 33, 48, 61,
    99, 109, 118
Aplomado Falcon, 33, 99
apteria, 72
Archaeopteryx, 94, 96

Bald Eagle, 87, 101, 125
Barn Owl, 47
Bat Falcon, 33
beak, 5
billing, 57
binocular vision, 27
Black Falcon, 99
Boke of Saint Albans, 107
boobies, 6
botanicals, 122
British Falconers' Club, 109
brood rearing, 3
buteo (soaring hawks), 88, 89
buzzard, 4, 89

California Condor, 9
cannibalism, 41
captive breeding, 118–121, 138
Caracara, 98, 101
carbamates, 124
Cathartidae, 87, 100, 101
Cenozoic, 96
cholinesterase, 123
Circus, 89
clutch, 63, 64
clutch size, 64
coloration, 5

Common Kestrel, 33
condor, 4, 6, 8
Cooper's Hawk, 30, 100
copulation, 59, 60, 61
courtship, 55–62
courtship feeding, 57
coverts, 92, 95
Cretaceous, 96
cryoprotectants, 121

DDT, 82, 121, 123, 124, 125, 126
De Arte Venandia cum Avibus,
    108
density, 12
Desert Falcon, 102
dieldrin, 123
diet, 34–44
disease, 51
dispersal, 17, 76, 77, 78, 79, 80
distribution, 10

eagle, 4, 88
ecological interactions, 45–52
egg color, 64
egg laying, 59, 61
egg mortality, 67
eggs, 8
eggshell, 94
eggshell thinning, 83
egg size, 64
egg turning, 64
Eleonora's Falcon, 29, 33
encephalitis, 51
European Kestrel, 19, 118
European Sparrow Hawk, 17
evolution, 94, 96, 98, 99